JOHN DANIEL

Scarlet and the Beast

III

ENGLISH FREEMASONRY, BANKS, AND THE ILLEGAL DRUG TRADE

ⓄMNIA VERITAS.

John Daniel

Scarlet and the Beast III
English Freemasonry, banks, and the illegal drug trade

First Edition, 1995 JKI Publishing Tyler, TX

© Omnia Veritas Limited - 2023

𝒪MNIA VERITAS®

www.omnia-veritas.com

CONTENTS

Preface

A General Overview

*S*carlet and the Beast, published in three volumes, is based on the prophecy of Jesus Christ as recorded by the Apostle John in Revelation 17 and 18. In these Scriptures, Christ details the machinations of two mysterious end-time word powers called Mystery Babylon and the Beast. I have given Mystery Babylon the name "Scarlet".

As the Scriptural name Mystery Babylon indicates, Scarlet is the harlot religious system inaugurated by Satan at ancient Babylon. The Beast, as described in Revelation 12:3 and 9, is the universal political system devised by Satan, which will culminate in the one-world government prophesied in Revelation 13. From their inception at Babylon until the present day, both systems have United the two powers of religion and state. This coalition or union of religion with government is what is called the "Babylonian system". It is this crucial alliance between religion and state that allows us to identify the modern headquarters of Mystery Babylon.

The global reach of this Satanic System is described in Revelation 17:1. Scarlet, we are told, is sitting "upon many Waters". Verse 15 of the same chapter explains what these Waters signify: "The Waters which thu sawest, where the whore sitteth, are peoples, and multitudes, and nations, and tongues." Clearly Scarlet is a religion that encompasses the whole Earth. In fact, her temples, which can be found in every nation of the world, total over nine Thousand. Three Thousand are in the kingdom where she claims citizenship, with 1,700 in the city from where she reigns.

Over the millenniums Scarlet has claimed many denominations and has been known by many names. Today, specifically in Western nations, these pagans, and even ostensibly Christian denominations, fall under the umbrella of what is called the new age movement. What is meant by the new age? The answer is found in astrology, whose adepts teach that there exists a time clock in the night sky called the zodiac. This great turning wheel of twelve constellations makes a complete rotation approximately every 24,000 years. Each of the twelve constellations, therefore, has ascendancy over the skies of the Earth for about 2,000 years. According to the ancient Babylonian astrologers, as each new constellation arrives a "new age" is born, accompanied by a catastrophic or otherwise crucial event on the Earth. Modern mystics of the pagan new age movement claim that the crucial event that ushered in the age of Pisces (the fishes) two Thousand years ago was the birth of Jesus Christ. Hence, in the year 2000, when Pisces succumbs to the ascendency of Aquarius, we can expect—according to new-agers—that Christianity will cease to exist and mankind will take a "quantum leap" into godhood, the final cycle of evolution.

Christians should recognize the pagan origins and nature of the new age creed as the same lie the Serpent whispered to Adam and Eve in the Garden of Eden: "ye shall be as gods" (Genesis 3:5). Throughout history, Satan has used this lie to seduce men and to enroll humanity in this attempt to dethrone the Almighty.

The three volumes of Scarlet and the Beast are my attempt to expose Satan's strategy and tactics in the modern era in his war against the throne of God. The respective subtitles of this three-book series are volume one: *A History of the War between English and French Freemasonry*; volume two: *English Freemasonry, Mother of Modern Cults vis-a-vis Mystery Babylon, Mother of Harlots*; and volume three: *English Freemasonry, Banks, and the Illegal Drug Trade*.

Volume I: The Political Wars

Volume I examines the origins and histories of these two malevolent powers that are contending for the political, religious, and financial control of the world. Drawing upon Scripture, Scarlet and the Beast: A History of the War between English and French Freemasonry documents the identities of Scarlet and the Beast: Scarlet is English Freemasonry, and the Beast will arise from French Freemasonry.

Scarlet and the Beast are adversaries. Whatever Scarlet is, the Beast is not. For example, the politics and economics of Scarlet are aristocratic, wealthy, capitalistic, and right-wing; in religion, she is pantheistic. The Beast, on the other hand, is proletarian, poor, socialistic, communistic, and left-wing: the Beast promotes atheism.

Volume I documents the conflict between these two powers that has played itself out in the revolutions of the last three centuries, as well as in the two World Wars of the twentieth century.

Scarlet can be found wherever Satan has established his Babylonian system of the union of religion and government. It is this union that identifies the westward movement of Mystery Babylon. Volume I tracks Scarlet's westward journey from Babylon to her present headquarters. The final chapter of this volume documents the headquarters of the Beast empire. The prophet Daniel and the Apostle John, in their descriptions of the Beast (Daniel 7:8 and Revelation 13:16-18), report what is a prominent Masonic symbol that doubles for the national emblem of a powerful nation that exists in our day.

Volume II: The Religious Wars

Scarlet is pantheistic in religion, demanding a belief in a Supreme Being, no matter what singular or multiple appellations it claims. The Beast, by contrast, has publicly declared its humanistic and atheistic position in religion since 1877, when it published a document stating that there is no personal god apart from humanity in total.

In an exploration based upon chapters 17 and 18 of Revelation, English Freemasonry, Mother of Modern Cults vis-a-vis Mystery Babylon, Mother of Harlots further documents Scarlet's role as modern Mystery Babylon. We return to ancient Babylon to witness how the Babylonian priesthood controlled monarchies and fomented revolutions in the same manner and for the same reason as does Freemasonry today. The rituals of ancient Babylonian religions are compared with those of Freemasonry and found to be identical. Finally, we discover the real identity of Melchizedek (Genesis 14:18), a powerful and godly monarch identified in Hebrews 6:20 as a type of Christ, who destroyed for a time the ancient religion of Babylon, forcing it underground to practice its wicked rites in secret caverns beneath the earth. "For this reason", say the votaries of Freemasonry, "we must remain a secret society today".

Volume III: The Financial Wars

English Freemasonry is wealthy and capitalistic, controlling the money and rulers of the world through banking and commerce. French Freemasonry, on the other hand, is poor and communistic, attempting to control state finances through an all-powerful socialistic government.

English Freemasonry, Banks, and the Illegal Drug Trade documents how English Freemasonry has acquired domination and control of world banking, including possession of most of the world's gold, and how today she is destroying the Judeo-Christian heritage of the West by financing the growth, manufacture, and trafficking of illegal drugs worldwide. This last book finds the Harlot's abominable cup in the hands of English Freemasonry.

Revelation 18:23 describes the servants and methods of the Harlot: "for thy merchants were the great men of the Earth; for by thy sorceries were all nations deceived." The Greek words for sorceries and sorcerers are used in the book of Revelation in a manner unlike any other place in Scripture. In Revelation 9:21, 18:23, 21:8, 22:15, the Greek words are pharmakeia, pharmakeus, pharmakon, and pharmakos, and refer only to Mystery Babylon and her one-world system. From these Greek words we receive such ordinary English words as pharmaceutical, pharmacy, and pharmacist.

The "real thing", according to the Witters, has nothing to do with calling on the revealed God of the Holy Bible to help in lifting the curse of drug addiction, but rather with petitioning pagan gods through mystic meditation to achieve the same euphoric state without the use of drugs. "Some people who meditate", confirm the Witters,

> "reach a deep state of relaxation and tranquility that is called satori… This systematized practice is what yoga, Sufism, Zen Buddhism, and other spiritual paths are about".

The Witters unwittingly confirm that the use of drugs in Western society has caused many to stray from Christian orthodoxy to Eastern and New Age mysticism:

> People who have not yet learned to meditate effectively continue to use drugs, because they seem to work immediately, whereas meditation requires regular, daily practice and some discipline, especially at first… Those who select the psychedelics, especially for spiritual and mystical experiences, might find greater appeal in studies of mysticism and meditation.

As we saw in volume one of *Scarlet and the Beast*, Eastern mysticism and our modern New Age movement are identical in nature. Just as mind-altering drugs were used to draw people into the pagan mystery religions of times past, so too are they used today: to entice and seduce people from the true religion of Christianity and draw them into worship in the harlot religion called Mystery Babylon.

Introduction

Drugs, the Occult, and Deception

Revelation 18:23 states of Mystery Babylon, "by thy sorceries were all nations deceived". As previously noted, the Greek word for sorceries means "a seller of spell-giving potion". Significantly, the Greek word for deceived means "to stray from orthodoxy or piety". By considering these two meanings, we are pointed toward the reason for the use of drugs in mystery Babylonian religions—to deceive mankind into straying from God's truth.

The use of drugs to produce an altered state of mind in religious worshipers can be traced back to ancient times.

Edith Miller in *Occult Theocrasy* (1933) documents how the ancient magi used various drugs and techniques to induce or produce the extraordinary or ecstatic:

> It would be impossible to enumerate the different drugs, ingredients and implements that compose the stock-in-trade of a magician... The standard Indian book on magic is the Oupnek'hat. Therein is to be found a detailed description of methods available for producing catalepsy, somnambulism, hallucination and ecstasy..."

A modern textbook for drug and alcohol abuse counselors, *Drugs and Society: A Biological Perspective* (1986), by Drs. Patricia and Weldon Witters, confirms that drugs have sometimes been used to create religious experience.

The Witters trace the use of drugs from ancient mystery religions to their recreational use in our day. The final chapter, subtitled

Using the Mind for Nondrug Highs, suggests that the alternative to drug addiction is to return to the practice of ancient mystic meditation:

Experimental psychiatrists, neurophysiologists, psychologists, and physicians are investigating the mind. Some of the most intriguing work is being done on the state of the mind during meditation. Countries like India have long histories linked to people who were able to achieve certain goals through meditation. The word yoga is derived from the Sanskrit word for union or yoking, meaning the process of discipline by which a person attains union with the Absolute. In a sense, it refers to the use of the mind to control itself and the body. Various systems of mind control have been used for thousands of years to find Peace and contentment within... These effects occur without drugs, but drugs can speed up the process tremendously, and often unpredictably.

The category of people who take drugs as part of their search for the meaning of life eventually look for other methods of maintaining the valuable parts of the drug experience. Such people learn to value the meditation "high" and abandon drugs. They describe their drug experiences as having given them a taste of their potential, as something they grew out of now that they are established in the real thing...

The "real thing", according to the Witters, has nothing to do with calling on the revealed God of the Holy Bible to help in lifting the curse of drug addiction, but rather with petitioning pagan gods through mystic meditation to achieve the same euphoric state without the use of drugs. "Some people who meditate", confirm the Witters,

> "reach a deep state of relaxation and tranquility that is called satori... This systematized practice is what yoga, Sufism, Zen Buddhism, and other spiritual paths are about".

The Witters unwittingly confirm that the use of drugs in Western society has caused many to stray from Christian orthodoxy to Eastern and New Age mysticism:

People who have not yet learned to meditate effectively continue to use drugs, because they seem to work immediately, whereas meditation requires regular, daily practice and some discipline, especially at first... Those who select the psychedelics, especially for spiritual and mystical experiences, might find greater appeal in studies of mysticism and meditation.

As we saw in volume one of Scarlet and the Beast, Eastern mysticism and our modern New Age movement are identical in nature. Just as mind-altering drugs were used to draw people into the pagan mystery religions of times past, so too are they used today: to entice and seduce people from the true religion of Christianity and draw them into worship in the harlot religion called Mystery Babylon.

Drugs and Gnosis

Drug use can be traced to the beginning of time when Adam and Eve were caretakers of the Garden of Eden. The Serpent promised Adam and Eve that their eyes would "be opened" (Genesis 3:5) if they ate of the fruit of the tree knowledge of good and evil. The key word in this passage is eyes, which in Hebrew can be translated "knowledge". Opened can be translated "broadened". That the Serpent promised Adam and Eve was that their knowledge would be broadened if they ate of the forbidden fruit. But the most foreboding aspect of this Scripture emerges from the fact that the Hebrew word for "eyes" is not plural, but singular. What the Serpent actually told Adam and Eve was that their "eye" would be broadened by knowledge. The "eye" that Scripture wants us to consider is not the physical organ of sight, but the eye of the mind or soul. This singular "eye" is called the "third eye" of clairvoyance in the Hindu religion, the eye of Osiris in Egypt, and the All-Seeing Eye in Freemasonry. J.R. Church in Guardians of the Grail puts it this way:

We know that neither Adam nor Eve were blind. So, this scripture is not referring to their physical eyes, but to their Mind's Eye! Satan was able to introduce them to the opening up of their mind's eye—today sometimes called centering, deep relaxation or meditation—which allows a "spirit" to enter and practice "mind control". The original temptation and deception that occurred in the Garden of Eden is no different than the tactics and subtleties that Satan uses today. The serpent still beguiles men to partake of forbidden fruit.

J.R. Church then suggests that the forbidden fruit consumed by Adam and Eve was a type of mind-altering drug:

"It could have been a narcotic extraction such as those used in mind-expanding drugs—mescaline, heroin, marijuana, etc … Mind altering drugs are used to open the mind-s eye—the all seeing eye of clairvoyant perception".

Rabbinical tradition also suggests that Adam and Eve were seduced to partake in the devil-s sorceries. The Zohar suggests that Adam and Eve ate not the forbidden fruit of the tree, but its leaves—which were poisonous. The leaves and/or fruit of many narcotic plants are considered poisonous, but when administered in low doses produce other effects. The belladonna plant, for example, has been used for thousands of years by poisoners, yet when the extract is ingested at low doses it can produce sedation. At high doses it can produce excitation, delirium, hallucinations and even death. The rabbis likewise ascribe an hallucinogenic experience to Adam and Eve upon their partaking of the leaves of the tree:

"(They saw) delusive images from the tree of which they had eaten…"

Genesis 3:7 tells us what awaited Adam and Eve after they ate of the fruit:

"And the eyes of them both were opened, and they knew that they were naked; and they sewed fig leaves together, and made themselves aprons."

By considering this passage in the light of the original meanings of the Hebrew words and according to rabbinical tradition, we can begin to see just how deluded Adam and Eve were by Satan's promise of becoming gods. The word naked in Hebrew comes from a primitive root word which means "to be cunning, usually in a bad sense; take crafty counsel, be prudent, deal subtilly (sic)". Rabbinical tradition assigns the same meaning to the passage by suggesting that Adam and Eve ate the leaves of the tree to make "themselves acquainted with all kinds of magical arts..." Afterwards, the rabbis say, they girded themselves with the same leaves as weapons, "for the purpose of self-protection".

Rabbinical tradition, therefore, teaches that Adam and Eve indulged in the magical arts, which would include the use of mind-altering drugs in an attempt to become gods. The two Hebrew words for leaves and apron certainly suggest the means and end of our first parents ungodly desire. Leaves is derived from the same primitive root word from which the word for Lucifer's reason comes. It means to "arise (up), (cause to) ascend up, climb (up), exalt, excel, (make to) rise (up), increase, leap, lift (self) up, mount up, (begin to) spring (up), grow (into), or work (toward). And the Hebrew word for aprons can also be translated "armor". That Adam and Eve girded themselves with the mind-altering leaves of the tree of the knowledge of good and evil may suggest humanity's continuing attempt to "work toward" becoming one with the Absolute through the ingestion of mind-altering drugs. This "armor" may have made Adam and Eve feel invincible— made them feel like gods.

We now see clearly the sin at Eden. It is more insidious than what our English translations convey. God commanded Adam and Eve not to eat of the pagan sacrament of the serpent. The ingestion of drugs would cause humanity, if not Adam and Eve, to stray further from orthodoxy and piety. If we understand the eating of the fruit of the tree of the knowledge of good and evil as a symbolic representation of all religions of magic and witchcraft, and of all gnostic ways of knowing and practices which involve the use of drugs, then we understand what Scripture warns us against in the story of humanity's first, tragic fall from grace at Eden. This ritual or sacrament of knowing good and evil opened our first parent's "third eye" to the world of witchcraft, enabling them to "know", or practice the religion of good and evil. Their rebellion denuded them of God's protection. As a result, they and their progeny would be susceptible to the perversion of true religion in their naked exposure to witchcraft. 1

Samuel 15:23 equates disobedience with false religions:

> "For rebellion is as the sin of witchcraft, and stubbornness is as iniquity and idolatry."

The Serpent's subtle practice of offering drugs to Adam and Eve to deceive them into straying from orthodoxy and piety has been the practice of mystery Babylonian religions since. This final volume of Scarlet and the Beast will document the use of drugs as the control mechanism of ancient and modern Mystery Babylon. The financing of the illegal drug trade is the primary apparatus used by English Freemasonry today to deceive the nations into straying from orthodoxy and piety (Revelation 18:23).

Chapter 1

Ancient Mystery Babylon and Drugs

References to the ritual use of drugs are scattered through the history of religions, and there is no doubt that the practice is ancient, its origins lost in prehistory.

Hallucinogens

Mind-altering drugs have always played a large part in the ceremonies of mystery religions. Even as common a reference work as the Encyclopaedia Britannica sketches how far back in time the cultic and religious uses of drugs reach:

Presumed ceremonial use of Cannabis among the Scythians in the 5th to 2nd century B.C. is suggested by the censers for burning hemp seeds found in the frozen tombs at Pazyryk in the Altai Mountains. The ancient Greeks used wine (laced with leaves from the belladonna plant) in Dionysian rites, and circumstantial evidence points to the use of an Eleusinian Mysteries of ancient Greece: the drinking of kykeon, a thick gruel of unknown composition.

Both the secular and the cultic use of the Amanita muscaria mushroom in Siberia probably go back more than 6,000 years, and cultic use has spread beyond the cool temperate climates where the mushroom grows. Evidence of the cultic use of opium in the eastern Mediterranean islands, in Greece, and among the Sumerians point to dates as early a 3000 B.C., though some of this evidence is disputed.

One of the pharmacological mysteries is the nature of the Zoroastrian haoma and the early Hindu soma, both sacred drinks made from plants. Their source may have been the Amanita muscari mushroom, the mind-affecting chemicals of which pass into the urine with their properties very little diminished; there are (Hindu) scriptural references to sacred urine drunk as the source of divine insights.

Sacred books themselves provide evidence of the use of drugs to enter into the "divine". The Hindu Rig Veda, Book VIII, 48 (Sanskrit hymns, 1500 B.c.), for instance, records a hymn to a mind-altering drink which brings the devotee to illumination and immortality—to godhood:

> We have drunk the Soma and become immortal!
> We have attained the light, we have found the Gods!
> What can the malice of mortal man or his spite,
> O Immortal, do to us now?

Another verse from the Rig Veda describes how the priests would urinate soma and drink it once again to alter their consciousness. Even today some Hindu priests in India consider their urine "holy water". Mahatma Gandhi (1869–1948), the India nationalist leader, deified urine and human excretion. The practice of drug ingestion from urine is found elsewhere in the world. In Siberia, for instance, "most of the hallucinogen (of the Amanita muscari mushroom) passes through the body and is excreted in the urine unchanged ... (so that) the lowliest servants could partake of the drug, although they had to get it second—, third—, or fourth-hand".

What were the effects of soma—the Hindu holy drink? Some researchers believe it caused hallucinations. Others believe the soma contained hashish, which creates a feeling of invincibility. In any case, those who ingested such drugs, in the history of religion, have claimed participation in, or communication with the sacred, or both. Often these persons are accorded the position of prophet, mystic, or magician:

Many people throughout the ages perceived a person who saw visions or experienced hallucinations as a holy or sacred individual, or possibly bewitched. There are many indications that some of the medicine men, shamans, witches, oracles, and perhaps mystics and priests of various groups knew how to induce hallucinogenic experiences.

(For example, the Jimsonweed, Datura stramonium, is) mentioned in early Sanskrit and Chinese writings and were revered by the Buddhists. There is also some indication that the priestess at the ancient Greek temple of Apollo at Delphi was under the influence of Datura when she made prophecies. Prior to the supposed divine possession, she appeared to have chewed leaves of the sacred laurel. There was also reported to be a mystic vapor that arose from a fissure in the ground. The sacred laurel may have been one of the Datura species and the vapors may have come from burning these plants...

We also know that the Assyrians sucked on opium lozenges, and that about 2000 years ago the Romans ate hashish sweets. In the western hemisphere, the oldest record found of hallucinogens is from a 4500-year-old grave of a South American Indian: beside him was a snuff tube. The ingredients in the tube were tested and found to be a fairly potent hallucinogen. The Indians from the region called it cohoba snuff. Likewise, the natives of Haiti claim that "under the influence of the (same) drug they can communicate with their gods".

In Central America more than 2000 years ago the hallucinogenic mushroom Psilocybe mexicana was used by the natives. In the 1500s, then the Spaniards arrived in Mexico, the Aztecs were using the Psilocybe mexicana mushroom for their ceremonial rites, referring to it as "God's flesh". Apparently, the ancient Aztecs and Mayan Indians also knew that certain varieties of morning glories had hallucinogenic properties. For example, when the priests wanted to commune with and receive messages from their gods, they ate the core of the morning glory, which includes the seeds of Rivea corymbosa, and which is still used today in divination and healing rituals in Oaxaca. In the 1500s the Spanish explorers reported that

> "the seeds were not reserved for the priests alone, but were medicinally to cure flatulence, to remove venereal troubles, to deaden pain, and to alleviate tremors".

In North America, mescaline, a hallucinogen from the peyote cactos, has been used for centuries. And because Native Americans believed that their gods created it as a special gift to commune more directly with them, this sacramental plant played a central role in their ceremonies. Padre de Leon, a Jesuit missionary to the American Indians, believed the natives used peyote to conjure up demons, and he demanded that his converts renounce its use.

Four hundred years later in the 1970s, when a Native American was convicted for using the mescaline from the peyote cactos, the Supreme Court heard the case and ruled that "Native Americans could use it within the confines of their religion".

LSD

The natural preparations used in the so-called "witches' brew" is thought to have been mescaline, for it induced the sensation of dissociation from the body, or flying or floating. A manufactured mescaline is lysergic acid diethylamide (LSD), a relatively new drug which has a potente effect on the brain and behavior. First manufactured to reproduce schizophrenic episodes for laboratory study, LSD rapidly proved itself ineffective in this respect and found its way to the streets. LSD creates the same sensation as the witches brew. The user may observe himself as two people, often experiencing the sensation that the mind and body are two separate entities. Low to médium doses of LSD produce na ecstatic state of euforia, followed by feelings of anxiety, and less frequently, by depression. These various effects are determined by purity or contamination of the drug. When manufactured in illegal laboratories, for example, LSD may contain dangerous, levels of strychnine.

LSD first became popular in academic, professional, and artistic circles during the 1950s. The drug gained notoriety in the early 1960s as a result of experimentation by Drs. Richard Alpert and Timothy Leary, two Harvard University psychology professor who invited others to "turn on, turn in, and drog out" of the existing social institutions.

These two men actually started a religion using LSD as a sacrament. Their book, The Psychedelic Experience, which is based on the Tibetan Book of the Dead, became the bible of the psychedelic drug movement.

Cocaine

Cocaine, a stimulant, also has been used for centuries. Evidence its earliest use was found at a Peruvian gravesite dating back to about 500 A.D., in which was found a supply of coca leaves. The carved surfaces of ancient Peruvian pottery show characteristic cheek bulges of the coca chewer. Natives of Peru, Bolivia, and Colombia have long used coca leaves for stimulation, or to combat fatigue. In the 16th century, when be Spaniards conquered the Incas, it was likewise discovered that coca leaves were used by these Indians in their religious ceremonies and in bartering.

As near as a century ago cocaine was not considered addictive, hence me drug was openly fashionable in Europe.

Famous men such as Robert Louis Stevenson and Sigmund Freud used cocaine almost daily. The drug first entered the United States of America in the latter half of the nineteenth century as a local anesthetic for eye surgery. Then in 1886, Dr. J.C. Pemberton created a concoction of liquids from extracts of the coca plant and the nuts of the cola plant. He named his new tonic Cola-Cola. Having difficulty marketing his brew as a therapeutic nerve tonic, the doctor publicized it as a stimulating soda fountain drink. In 1903 the use of cocaine in Coca-Cola was discontinued.

Today cocaine is legally classified as a narcotic, although its action is just the opposite to that or a narcotic. Instead of sedating the user, as does a narcotic, cocaine induces intense euphoric and hallucinatory effects for a short period of time.

Opiates

The opiate narcotics group includes those drugs that are derivatives of, or are pharmacologically related to, products from the opium poppy plant. The best known opiates are heroin, morphine, and codeine. There are also many synthetic opiates, such as heroin, methadone, and propoxyphene (Darvocet). These drugs are used medically primarily for their analgesic (pain relief) qualities. Some are used to suppress coughing and to stop diarrhea. Most of these drugs are strongly addictive.

Opium, a depressant, is the oldest narcotic known to man. We can date its use to 6000 years ago from references in Sumerian tablets. The Sumerians called poppy the "joy plant." The Egyptians also made mention of it about 1500 B.C., and the Greeks about 1000 B.C. In fact, the Greek and Roman gods of sleep, Hypnos and Somnus, were portrayed as carrying a container of opium pods, while the Minoan goddess of sleep wore a crown of opium pods.

Poppy was so important to Greek culture that the opium pod was imprinted on their gold coins. And according to Greek mythology, the poppy was sacred to Demeter, the goddess of sowing and reaping, and to her daughter Persephone. In the first century A.D., a technique to extract opium from the poppy pod was developed. In 1803 the addictive potential of opium was significantly increased when, in Germany, a way to extract the poppy's active ingredient was discovered. The extraction was called morphine, named after the Greek god of dreams, Morpheus.

Morphine was ten times more potent than opium. Finally, in 1898, chemists at Bayer Laboratories found that by adding two acetyl side groups to the morphine molecule an even more potent compound they named heroin would be formed. Although the most addictive of the opiates, heroin was advertised by Bayer as "a heroic drug, without the addictive potential of morphine." Heroin received its name from the word "heroic" in this advertisement. In 1924, heroin was banned from American medicine. It is now a Schedule I drug, with a high potential for abuse and no currently accepted medical use.

Marijuana

Marijuana is a milder drug than that produced by the poppy and coca plants. It is often called hemp, because the woody fibers of the stem can be made into cloth and rope. In 1753, Carolus Linnaeus, a Swedish botanist, classified marijuana as Cannabis sativa. The term cannabis comes from the Greek word for hemp. The oldest mention of marijuana use is found in the book of drugs, written about 2737 B.C. by the Chinese Emperor Shen Nung. Cannabis was prescribed as a medicinal drug for the treatment of gout, malaria, gas pains, and absentmindedness. Although marijuana continued to be used in China for medical treatment, the plant got a bad name from the moralists around 500 B.C., who claimed that youngsters became wild and disrespectful from its recreational use. Children would actually refuse to listen to their elders, and they engaged in other scandalous activities while under the influence of marijuana. It was banned at that time but later legalized. In India, Hindus used marijuana for thousands of years as an essential part of religious ceremonies. The Rig Veda and other Hindu hymns describe the use of soma, which some speculate was marijuana. For centuries missionaries in India have tried to ban it, but they were unsuccessful because its use was so heavily ingrained in the culture.

Drugs, Religion, and Sex

Another application of drugs which we can trace back to antiquity is their use as aphrodisiacs in religious ceremonies. Certain drugs known as "love potions" were employed by priests and priestesses in their religious rituals in connection with rites characterized by sexual excesses. Two such drugs extracted from the belladonna and henbane plants are hyoscyamine and scopolamine. They were used at the Bacchanalia, the annual drunken feast in honor of the Greek god Bacchus, which climaxed in a sexual frenzy. Wild-eyed priestesses with flowing locks, flung themselves naked into the arms of eager men. The wine with which the Bacchante had become intoxicated was doctored with the leaves or berries of the belladonna or henbane plants. (The species name, belladona, means "beautiful woman.")

These two drugs were also known as "witches' potions" and were used in the Black Mass, or Sabbat. In this fertility rite, witches smeared a wooden phallus or dildo with the potion and inserted it into their vagina. Soon the active ingredient was absorbed into the bloodstream through the vaginal wall, giving the participants a sensation or being carried in the air as they Jumped over fire. Some women who took part in these rituals brought their brooms as anointed phallic symbols. Inserting them into their vagina, then jumping over the fire, gave rise to the idea that witches ride broomsticks.

Most or the new witches and warlocks of our era practice satanism and use similar drugs, serving them as wine and wafers at their Black Masses. One of the high priestesses ferreted out for Esquire magazine says,

> "I give acid to persons who have never dropped it without telling them. I think of this as the administering of Holy Communion."

Members of these covens tell of enjoying all the sensations which have been common to such groups since medieval times, such as out-of-body travel, illusions of flight, supreme sexual force, and the gift of magical power to destroy one's enemies. Female members have even admitted to having had hallucinatory sexual relations with Satan, a notorious phenomenon of witchcraft throughout the ages.

Likewise, the use of drugs-for-sex in some of the English Masonic Lodges was prolific at the beginning of the twentieth century. For example, the Masonic lodges founded by 33rd degree English Freemason Aleister Crowley were in truth nothing more than dope dens and whore-houses. When Crowley split off from the Masonic sex lodge, Order of the Golden Dawn to form the Stella Matutina, he continued the rituals of the former where the consumption of hashish was combined with sexual perversion.

The same drug culture dominated the Masonic lodges in France during the 1840s, where the use of hashish, as well as opium, was widespread, and efforts to curb its use were unsuccessful. During that time a group of popular literary people and artists in France formed the Club des Hachichins, the purpose of which was the search for new experiences and impressions of life. Such notable writers as Theophile Gautier, Charles Baudelaire, and Alexandre Dumas were regular members. Dumas, most famous today for The Three Musketeers, was a Mason noted in his day for bringing a contemporary drama of adultery and honor to the stage. It is possible that the other two men were Masons as well, since they followed the Masonic line in their writings. Gauder, for example, was a proponent of nihilism, while the poetry of Baudelaire was both obscene and blasphemous.

Prior to the French Revolution, that great Masonic organizer Cagliostro also used drugs to deceive. Dr. George E. Dillon in Grand Orient Freemasonry Unmasked (1885) writes that

> "Cagliostro claimed the power of conferring immortal youth, health, and beauty, and what he called moral and physical regeneration, by the aid of drugs and Illuminated Masonry."

Drugs for Assassination

Mystery Babylon has not only used drugs to deceive the masses into joining its licentious religion, but it has employed them as poisons to eliminate enemies. We recall that one of the definitions for sorcerer (Revelation 18:23) is "poisoner." The Greeks, for example, used the deadly drug produced from the Atropa plant to do away with their enemies. The name given the plant indicates the reverence the Greeks had for it:

> "Atropos was one of the three Fates in Greek mythology, whose duty it was to cut the thread of life when the time came. This plant was one used for thousands of years by poisoners."

From the fourteenth through the sixteenth centuries A.D. the Rosicrucians were great manufacturers of poisons.

A secret society that was a forerunner to English Freemasonry was the Rosicrucians, the first of modern drugs experimenters. As alchemists in search of the magic potion to prolong life, known as the "elixir of long life," Rosicrucians expanded the development of mind-altering drugs. Rosicrucians were also the first modern secret society to be politically involved in revolution, and hence were accused of many assassinations by use of poisons.

How many political and religious leaders in the last 150 years have been poisoned for standing in the way of Masonic progress may never be known, but three documented illustrations follow.

During the Italian Revolution in the 1860s, 33rd degree Mason Joseph Mazzini, founder of the Mafia, used poisons extensively to assassinate his opponents. He sent Freemason Francesco Crispi to France to assassinate Napoleon III, but Crispi failed. Early in April 1862, while attending a freemasonic dinner, Crispi himself was poisoned as a traitor to the revolution. After taking the poison, which had been administered in his bread, fire seemed to be burning within him. Those in attendance began to laugh. One rose and spoke to him severely in the following terms:

> Francesco, you went to visit King Victor Emmanuel, without telling us of your intentions and you offered him your secret services. You let him know that you were ready to go over at the first opportunity. Till then your opinions had been republican. Well, that is treason. We have condemned you. You are poisoned. You are a dead man.

In our day poisons are still being used by Freemasonry to eliminate its opponents. You may recall in volume one of Scarlet and the Beast that when the Masonic-controlled Pope Paul VI (Giovanni Battista Montini) died on August 6, 1978, his successor, Albino Luciani, took the name John Paul I. The new pope's immediate agenda was to retire twenty-two bishops and cardinals in the Vatican who had joined the Mafia-run P-2 Masonic Lodge. John Paul had discovered that the Vatican bank, under the presidency or Freemason Bishop Marcinkus, was laundering Mafia drug money. Luciani lasted 33 days. It is believed by investigative journalist David A. Yallop that Pope John Paul I was poisoned by an overdose of digitalis on the orders of Italian Freemasonry. Digitalis was introduced in the early nineteenth century by 33rd degree French Freemason Pierre G. Vassal (1769–1840) as a treatment of diseases of the heart. It is difficult to detect poisoning by digitalis, because when taken in excess it gives the symptoms of a heart attack.

Most recent is the story of Rev. Ed Decker, who runs a Christian mission in the northwestern United States called "Free the Masons Ministries." In March 1986 Decker was touring Scotland and lecturing against Freemasonry. His host became nervous when two men invited them to eat at a downtown pizza shop. Decker recalls that "during the meal, one of them motioned to my empty coke glass and jumped up to bring a refill. He didn't offer to fill anyone else's glass." Rev. Decker drank the coke and within the hour was stricken with severe stomach pains and diarrhea. When he was finally taken to the hospital the doctors diagnosed acute arsenic poisoning and administered an antidote. Ed Decker lived to tell his story.

But assassinations involving drugs have occurred centuries before the days of Rosicrucianism and Freemasonry.

In 1090 A.D., the Persian Hasan Saba founded a secret society called Hashishiyin or Assassins. Edith Miller in Occult Theocrasy informs us that "the term Assassins is a corruption of Hashishim, derived from Hashish [Indian hemp] with which the chief intoxicated his followers when they entered on some desperate enterprise." Several medieval European kings were suspected of hiring the Assassins to rid themselves of their enemies. The nephew of Barbarossa, Frederick Il (king of Sicily 1198–1250), for example, was excommunicated by Pope Innocent Il (1130–1143) for having caused the Duke of Bavaria to be slain by the Assassins.

Today, the Mafia, a creation of Italian Freemasonry, follows the tradition of the Assassins with both dagger and poison. In a later chapter we will discuss how the Masonic Mafia is used by contemporary English Freemasonry for assassinations and drug running.

As Revelation 18:23 states, Mystery Babylon is in control of the universal distribution of mind-altering drugs to both deceive the nations into straying from the Christian faith, and to poison those who slow the progress of inaugurating its one-world government. English Freemasonry is Mystery Babylon's modern name. We shall now learn how the British Brotherhood got started in her universal drug trafficking business.

Chapter 2

Modern Mystery Babylon and Drugs

The Chinese Opium Wars: A Blueprint for America

As long as this country maintains its drug traffic, there is not the slightest possibility that it will ever become a military threat, since the habit saps the vitality of the nation.

So spoke a leading drug trafficker in a letter to his superiors. Although the trafficker could well have been describing America, he is not referring to the United States, but to China in 1838, on the eve of the first Opium War when Great Britain landed troops to compel Chinese to ingest the poison distributed by British merchants.

Four years later in 1842, Great Britain's army of ten thousand soldiers had won a victory over 350 million Chinese.

London's military success against the Chinese was not due to superior military advantage, but to its strategy between 1830–1839 of decimating the Chinese army through drug addiction.

This famous cartoon, reproduced here, dates back to the 1839 Opium War, and shows a British military man shoving opium down the throat of a Chinaman.

British Merchants of the Earth

The vehicle by which London shipped her drugs to China and elsewhere around the world was founded in 1600.

Capriciously called "Dope. Inc.", the British East India Company (BEIC) was incorporated by royal charter on December 31, 1600, under the name "Governor and Company of Merchants of London trading with the East Indies." Begun as a monopolistic trading body, the DEIC became involved in politics and acted as an agent of British imperialism in India starting in the mid-eighteenth century.

From its earliest years, the British East India Company was involved in Masonic revolutions, specifically Oliver Cromwell's Rosicrucian-Masonic insurrection against the Stuart monarchy. At first Cromwell dissolved all crown-protected monopolies, but finding his protectorate short of capital, he granted the BEIC a new charter in October of 1657 in return for financial aid.

The BEIC was not just another monopoly, but a Masonic monopoly. According to Dr. John Coleman, a former British intelligence officer,

> "to operate a trading company within the BEIC, the merchant must first be a Freemason or an initiate in one of its adjunct orders; and second, he must be given permission to join by the BEIC stockholders".

Initially the BEIC received tea, spices, and silks from the Orient return for fabrics manufactured from cotton grown on the southern plantations in the newly colonized Americas. As the ships sailed on their return from the Orient, they dropped anchor off the coast of Africa to board captured blacks who they would sell as slaves to work the cotton fields on the east coast of America. The use of slave labor enabled BEIC stockholders to maintain low overhead in their cotton production. Merchant families and plantation owners rapidly accumulated great wealth.

Prior to the American Civil War, the same British trading companies behind the slave trade in the South were running large numbers of Chinese indentured servants to the West Coast. This was called the "coolie trade" or "pig trade" by its British Hong Kong and Shanghai sponsors. The term "Shanghaied" has its origin in kidnapping drug addicted Chinese, who were boarded on BEIC ships at the port of Shanghai, and then shipped to the West Coast of the United States of America to be sold as indentured servants. These Chinese were the first buyers in the BEIC drug market in the western hemisphere, and as addicts, they simultaneously served as the initial means for trafficking in America.

The only competition the BEIC faced was from other nations such as France and the Netherlands, which also formed East India companies. The Dutch were unable to compete with the British and eventually gave England their trade rights to India. This gave the BEIC exclusive control of the entire opium trade in India, whose farmers produced the largest drug crop in the world. Through a strong advertising program, the BEIC encouraged the sale of tea while rapidly and energetically expanding its spice trade. Expanding revenues from tea made it possible for the English to colonize India, the garden spot of the world for poppy. Poppy juice, called opium, was extracted from the poppy and transported to China by the BEIC. It was this drug that helped bring on the Opium Wars in the mid-1800s, which further benefited British colonialism.

America was involved in the opium trade through Freemason John Jacob Astor, founder of the New York Astor family dynasty during the Revolutionary era. Astor was granted the privilege of becoming a BEIC stockholder and was one of the pioneers of the opium trade in China. However, opium was not a regular article of import into China by Americans until about 1816, four years after England made her first attempt to recapture America in the War of 1812.

In addition to the Astor group in New York City, the British East India Company developed similar networks in Philadelphia and Boston. Today these wealthy family networks have developed into what is called the "Eastern Establishment," which is headquartered in the Northern Jurisdiction of Scottish Rite Freemasonry at Boston, which stayed loyal to the British Crown following the American Revolution and the War of 1812.

A direct descendant of John Jacob Astor was American citizen Waldorf Astor, of Waldorf Astoria Hotel fame.

Waldorf Astor, a high-degree Mason in the Northern Jurisdiction of Scottish Rite Freemasonry, was, after World War Il, made chairman of the Royal Institute of International Affairs (RILA), which oversees the worldwide distribution of drugs for English Freemasonry. The counterpart of the RIIA in America is the Council on Foreign Relations (CFR), founded on July 29, 1921. In 1973 the CFR created the Trilateral Commission (TC) to establish tighter control over America's industries and financial institutions. (These organizations are the political arm of English Freemasonry in America, and will be discussed in more detail in the next chapter.)

Another American family which made its fortune in Chinese opium was the Freemasonic Delano family of the American Civil War era. Warren Delano, head of a China trading company in the mid-1800s, was the biggest U.S. dealer in opium. In a 1986 story on the history of drugs in America, the U.S. News & World Report said that "Delano equated the opium trade with the liquor business—both profitable and both the cornerstones of great family fortunes." Moreover, "Eleanor Roosevelt admitted in 1953 that the Delanos, 'like everybody else, had to include a limited amount of opium in their cargoes.'" Warren Delano's grandson was 32nd degree Freemason Franklin Delano Roosevelt, the three-term President who stacked the Supreme Court with a majority of Freemasons.

Other American families involved in the opium trade were the Sutherlands, Mathesons, Barings, and Lehmang.

The Sutherland family, one of the largest cotton and opium traders in the South, were first cousins to the Matheson family of Jardine Matheson, now one or the largest Hong Kong banking families financing the growing and distribution of the drugs in the Orient. The Barings founded the Peninsular and Orient Steam Navigation Company that transported opium from the Orient. The Freemasonic Rothschild family, as well as their New York banking cousins, the Lehmans of Lehman Brothers, all made their initial entry into the United States through the pre-Civil War cotton, drug, and slave trade.

English Freemasonry's Bid for Global Control of Narcotics

As we learned in volume one of Scarlet and the Beast, whether the English or the French have controlled the politics of any nation during the last two hundred years has been determined by which of the two opposing Masonic powers has had the most lodges in any given nation. The American Revolution, for example, was successful against the British because there were more French Masonic lodges in America than English. It was from French Masonic lodges that the American Revolution was plotted. While the French were chartering greater numbers of lodges throughout the continent of Europe and the New World, London was concentrating on the Orient. Wherever the BEIC traveled, its merchant shippers, doubling as the British Army and Navy, left behind a wake of English-chartered Masonic Lodges in the Far East. Mackey's *Encyclopedia of Freemasonry* confirms that "it will thus be seen that the planting of the Craft in India [was] by English merchants, soldiers, and sailors first.

Mackey details the development of British Freemasonry in India. George Pomfret, the first Provincial Grand Master of East India, was appointed in 1728. Captain Ralph Farwinter succeeded him the following year. In 1730 Farwinter constituted Lodge no. 72 in Bengal. The first Lodge on the Coast of Coromandel was established at Madras in 1752. A military lodge was chartered at Ceylon in 1761. Lodge no. 234 was constituted at Bombay in 1758, and Lodge no. 569 at Surat in 1798. According to Mackey, planting lodges in India coincided with the period of planting lodges in America. This was not coincidental, for Mackey confirms that the lodges established on both continents, on opposite sides of the earth, were chartered by the same English merchants, soldiers, and sailors.

The 1750s also saw the development and expansion of the worldwide missionary movements of Protestant denominations. In India, where drug use was a religious rite in the Hindu religion, Christian missionary activity was curtailed by the BEIC. The *Encyclopaedia Britannica* confirms that

> "the British East India company, conscious of the disadvantages of unnecessarily antagonizing its Indian subjects, excluded all Christian missionary activity from its territories. Indeed, the Company continued the patronage accorded by indigenous rulers to many Hindu temples and positively forbade its Indian troops to embrace Christianity."

Not only did the British repress Christian activity in India, London initially forbade Indian nationals, who were considered inferior to the white race, to join Freemasonry. According to Mackey, it was

> "not until long afterwards and then in small numbers only that they began to be admitted into membership."

The decision to admit Indians into Freemasonry was made a half-century prior to the first Chinese Opium War in 1840. The purpose of admission was to educate discretely a select group of Indian nationals in London's plan to ship an ever-increasing supply of drugs from India to China. Once destabilized, the vast and wealthy Chinese empire could be easily stripped of its wealth.

China: The First Drug Market for London

Freemason Thomas Robert Malthus (1766–1834), one of the initiators of British race patriotism, was the first to warn about the overpopulation of the world, especially from the proliferation of the dark-skinned races. The latter half of the nineteenth century saw a renewed interest in British race patriotism when Masonic economist John Stuart Mill (1806–1873) took up the cause of Thomas Malthus.

During the days of Malthus and Mill, the British race patriots taught that the Aryan race (i.e, light-skinned, blue-eyed, and blond people) was God's gift to the world. To save mankind from self-destruction, it was taught that the duty of British race patriots was to bring into subjection the ignorant, dark-skinned races. Thereafter, British colonialism no longer was considered a means of territorial expansion, but rather a means of the expansion of the white race at the expense of the dark-skinned nationals and their homelands. This, in turn, gave justification to strip the assets of every nation occupied by the British colonialists. It was during this time that the word "liberalism" was coined by the BEIC to defend the "freedom" of the British Masonic Oligarchy to loot the world of its assets. Colonialism and asset stripping of a nation became synonymous a century before the First Chinese Opium War in 1840.

The primary tool used by London to strip a nation of its assets was, and still is, to a war on that nation. Not only does widespread drug use weaken the moral fiber or an empire and its vitality to fight, it also strips it of hard currency. For example, between 1829 and 1840, a total of seven million silver dollars entered China, while 56 million silver dollars were sucked out by the soaring opium trade. These were published figures for the decade leading up to the First Opium war; however, this kind of asset-stripping had already been going on for a century.

Moreover, it was during this same century that London was planting lodges in India and the Americas as part of its grand scheme to fund the growth of the British empire and its white race. The authors of Dope, Inc. explain how opium played a vital role in London's success:

Opium was the final stage in the demand cycle for British financed and slave-produced cotton. British firms brought cotton to Liverpool. From there, it was spun and worked up in cloth in the mills in the north of England, employing unskilled child and female labor at extremely low wages. The finished cotton goods were then exported to India… India paid for its imported cloth … with the proceeds of Bengali opium exports to China.

Without the "final demand" of Chinese opium sales, the entire world structure of British trade would have collapsed.

It is around the slave production and transport of cotton that Britain gathered allies in the United States into the orbit of the East India Company's opium trade cycle.

Beginning in 1729, the British exploited an already drug-addicted China. The Witters sketch the development of drug addiction in China up to this decisive year:

During the so-called Dark Ages that followed the collapse of the Roman Empire, Arab traders were actively engaged in traveling the overland caravan routes to China and to India, where they introduced opium. Eventually those two countries grew their own opium poppies.

The opium poppy was a factor in a drastic change that took place in China: widespread drug addiction among its population... At first the seeds, and later opium, were used medically. Recreational use was not a problem until the introduction of opium smoking in the late 1690s... The Chinese government, fearful of the weakening of national vitality by ... drugs ... especially the potent opiate, forbade their use by the people. In 1729 China outlawed the sale or opium; the penalty was death by strangulation?

By imperial edict China closed its ports to "free trade" in 1729 in an attempt to curtail the flow of England's disastrous drug traffic. Free trade and the increase of drug trafficking go hand-in-hand, for free trade means limited inspections or none at borders. Closing the borders, however, did not hamper Great Britain's lucrative drug trade for two reasons. First, the imperial power of China was failing; for the next four decades it was unable to enforce the ban. Second, the Masonic BEIC had already made arrangements with the Chinese Triads, a vicious hodgepodge of secret societies similar to western Freemasonry, to smuggle the drugs across Chinese borders.

British Masonic Drug Lodges and the Triad Societies

To establish a beachhead on Chinese soil, English Freemasonry chartered its first Masonic lodge in the port city of Canton in 1767 (Amity Lodge No. 407). Over the next six years the British East India Company substantially increased its illegal opium imports to China by selling the drugs to the Triads, who then smuggled them from port warehouses into inland China. By 1773, the burgeoning demand for opium was so great that the British colonial government of India granted the BEIC an exclusive monopoly over the entire Indian poppy crop to meet Chinese demand. It was at this time that the British began to initiate Indian nationals into Freemasonry. With these Indian lodges and the Chinese mad societies, London declared a secret drug war on China.

A History of the Triad Societies

Secret societies have long played an integral role in the history of China. An old Chinese saying reads, "The officials draw their power from the Law, the people from the Secret Societies."

Of the many secret societies that have existed in China, none has wielded greater power than the triad group.

They are mentioned in nearly every history of the Chinese people. Like Freemasons, their members are bound together by an intricate system of secret rituals, oaths, and passwords. And like Freemasonry, they actually were a brotherhood for freedom. For example, they led many brave, but abortive uprisings against the Manchu emperors, who retaliated with even more than usual oriental ruthlessness. Fenton Bresler in The Chinese Mafia (1984) explains:

Just as the Mafia was founded by (Freemason) Giuseppe Mazzini in Palermo, Sicily in 1860 as a guerilla force to drive out a foreign ruler and unite with mainland Italy in the name of patriotism and liberty, so the earliest Triad Societies came into existence in Fukien Province in the latter part of the seventeenth century as valiant resistance fighters against the alien oppression of the Manchus, "barbarian" tribesmen who had swept across the Great Wall of China and in 1644 defeated the ruling native Ming Dynasty of Emperors to set up their own Ch'ing Dynasty."

Legend traces the founding of the first Triad Society to a militant group of Buddhist monks at a monastery near Foochow in Fukien Province in 1674. Their monastery was a rallying-point against the Manchus, and the monks practiced a highly specialized form of physical self-defense that they had perfected for themselves—Kung Fu.

The Triad's activities also had a darker side. Like the Italian Masonic Mafia, the Triads directly, or through subsidiaries, controlled much of the gambling, robbery and prostitution enterprises in China and in overseas Chinese communities. Like the Freemasons, they were unmatched in politics. In imperial China, the Triads were the principal instrument for the expression of political grievances. And like Freemasonry, it was the mad Societies who won the political fortunes of the republic, whose most famous president was mad member General Chiang Kai-shek.

Hong Kong police officer W.P. Morgan observed in 1960 that

> "the assistance given by the Triad Society to the Republicans resulted in its virtual official recognition by the new government and, free from restrictions, it expanded to an even greater extent than before. Its power as a lobbying force became such that ambitious civic and military officials were usually bound to join the society in order to further their ends, and merchants and traders found membership and subscriptions to the society greatly eased their commercial ventures."

The Triad societies were fit companions for the Freemasonic British East India Company. This "Chinese Mafia" taught the

English Freemasons how to subvert the Chinese government and thus bypass the drug control laws meant to suppress and eliminate opium use. And it was the Triads' underworld drug-dealing knowledge that was carried back in 1860 by those same English Masons to Freemason Joseph Mazzini and his Sicilian Mafia. With assistance from the Triads, opium imports into China kept rising in the name of British commercial enterprise.

Fenton Bresler in The Chinese Mafia picks up the story:

> Successive emperors pronounced further bans on the traffic in 1796, 1800, 1813 and 1815 but all to no avail. The situation became intolerable. The Chinese government demanded the right to regulate trade into its own country and protect its own subjects, the British demanded recognition of the right to do exactly what they wanted.

In blatant disobedience of the 1729 edict and its successors, and with the services of the Triads under the compulsion of "Masonic Brotherhood," the British East India Company increased the amount of opium entering China from 200 chests in 1729, to 30,000 to 40,000 chests (about 130 lbs. each) in 1838. Throughout the eighteenth century, a complex network of drug-smuggling secret societies were developed on mainland China with the help of local officials, who pocketed bribes from the smugglers. The Masonic-controlled BEIC shipped the drugs from India to their port in Canton. From there Triad gangs smuggled the drugs out of the warehouse area into the pores of the communities. And like the Italian Mafia one hundred years later, if any of their members or government officials got out of line they were ruthlessly eliminated.

While a succession of failing emperors helplessly watched the debauch of the population and the theft of their nation's assets, everyone beneath them was making money in the illegal drug trade. By 1829, a full century after the 1729 drug control edict, uncontrolled drug traffic was creating such severe trade deficits that Imperial China got serious about drug addiction and ordered the strict enforcement of the century-old edict against importation. The Emperor sent an honest and vigorous official, Imperial Commissioner Lin Tse-Hsu, to Canton to handle the problem. Lin demanded that the foreign importers surrender their stores and cargoes of opium. When the British traders refused, he threatened the Chinese merchants who were illegally trading in opium. When his warnings were repeatedly ignored. Lin burned 20,291 chests of opium in 1830, a hoard valued at $2 million.

The strict enforcement in 1829 by the Chinese government of its successive drug control edicts, and the 1830 prohibition of free trade created a crisis for London. The destruction by Lin Tse-Hsu of the Warehoused opium inventory was only a temporary financial blow. The long-term commercial implications to England, if the imperial commissioner's order were allowed to stand, was enormous. England's economic survival was at stake. London could not permit her lucrative drug trade to be curtailed. Her worldwide commercial expansion required it and funds to recapture the Americas it. England must go to war. But, how could Great Britain defeat an oriental nation on the far side of the globe, numbering 350 million people?

Communications criss-crossed the oceans. A drug trafficker assured his London superiors that "as long as this country (China) maintains it is drug traffic, there is not the slightest possibility that it will ever become a military threat, since the habit saps the vitality of the nation." Hence, the British garrison at Canton was given orders to force drugs down the throats of the Chinese until the Imperial Army was decimated by drug addiction.

In preparation for war, the BEIC opened in 1839 its first Masonic lodge at Basrah (in present-day southern Iraqi), to function as a center for Great Britain's intelligence operations under the guise of "pan-Islamism" or "pan-Arabism." Over the next three decades intelligence lodges were established at every port where the BEIC landed.

These British Masonic outposts served two purposes: (1) to keep the colonial governments in the East abreast of any potential

American-type revolution; and (2) to control the movement of drug traffic to the West.

Meanwhile, as war plans were discussed at Canton in 1838, the BEIC sent a memorandum to Freemason Henry Palmerston, the British Foreign Secretary, requesting that the Emperor be forced to agree to "(1) full legalization of opium trade into China; (2) compensation for the opium stockpiles confiscated by Lin to the tune of $2 million; and (3) territorial sovereignty for the British Crown over several designated offshore islands. In a simultaneous memorandum to Palmerston, Jardine placed J&M's [Jardine and Mathesons] entire opium fleet at the disposal of the Crown to pursue war against China.

Convinced that the time was right, Great Britain sent 10,000 troops to lay siege to Chinese ports in June of 1840.

Decimated by ten years of rampant opium addiction within the Imperial Army, the Chinese forces proved no match for the British.

Palmerston maintained constant communication with the war effort. Confident of victory, he sent a message in January 1841 to Freemason Lord Auckland, then Governor General of India, informing him of Britain's desire to increase opium production after the war. Following is an excerpt from that communication: The rivalship of European manufacturers is fast excluding our productions from the markets of Europe, and we must unremittingly endeavor to find in other parts of the world new vents for our industry (opium)... If we succeed in our China expedition, Abyssinia, Arabia, the countries of the Indus and the new markets of China will at no distant period give us a most important extension to the range of our foreign commerce (of opium)...

While the British fleet encountered a few difficulties in Canton, its threat to the northern cities, particularly Nanking, forced the Emperor to terms. Painfully aware that any prolonged conflict would merely strengthen Britain's bargaining position, the

Emperor petitioned for a treaty to end the war. In 1841, Crown Commissioner Captain Charles Elliot went to the negotiating table with the Emperor. He had orders from Freemason Lord Palmerston to demand admission of opium into China as an article of lawful commerce, increase indemnity payment, cede Hong Kong island to British colonial rule, and give the British access to several additional Chinese ports.

Bowing to a superior sovereign, the Emperor had no choice but to see his beloved China further impoverished.

The Treaty of Nanking, signed in 1842, brought the British Crown an incredible sum of Z21 million, as well as extraterritorial control over the "free port" of Hong Kong, which to this day is the capital of Great Britain's global drug running operations. The only drawback of the treaty was the requirement that British opium merchants pay import duties, which created onerous bookkeeping and tax burdens to the Masons who were accustomed to the illegal drug trade.

The First Opium War solidified the production and proliferation of drugs. The profiteering from mind-altering drugs became a cornerstone of British imperial policy. The drug trade was managed by English Freemasonry's far eastern lodges, which were strategically chartered throughout China following the war. The Royal Sussex Lodge, No. 735, for instance, was warranted at Canton in 1844. In 1847 Samuel Rawson was appointed Provincial Grand Master for China. All in all, the Grand Lodge of England established lodges in southern China at Amoy, Canton, Foochow, Swatow, and five at Hong Kong. In northern China, lodges were chartered at Chefoo, Chinkiang, Hankow, Newchang, Tongshan, Wei-Hai-Wei, two at Tientsin, and three at Shanghai. Before the ink was dry on the Treaty of Nanking, the British opium merchants began complaining about the bookkeeping overhead created by import duties. In response to their complaints, the British Crown precipitated events that would culminate in the Second Opium War against China in 1856, with similar disastrous consequences for the Chinese and with monumental profits for London's drug traffickers. Meanwhile

Lord Palmerston had attained the 33rd degree in Freemasonry; he had also been elected Prime Minister of England. As High Priest of English Freemasonry and head of British policy, he launched the Second Opium War in 1856, thereby fulfilling the "open China" policy he had outlined fifteen years earlier as Foreign Secretary.

In 1860 the British completed the process of opening all of China to the opium trade. That year the British East India Company turned over to the Triads the shipping of drugs into China and went into "legitimate business" by incorporating merchant banks and trading companies on the island of Hong Kong and the port of Shanghai under the corporate name of the Hong Kong & Shanghai Corporation. Banking became the primary source of "legitimate" revenue for the Masonic oligarchy; revenue that was generated by the financing of poppy farmers, drug manufacturers, and the laundering of dirty drug money deposited by the Triads. The British East India Company was no longer needed by English Freemasonry's "merchants of the earth." It went into decline and in 1873 was dissolved. To this day, the banks of the former Masonic stockholders of the BEIC serve as the central clearing house for all Far Eastern financial transactions relating to the black market in opium and its heroin derivative.

These financial transactions were, and are still, made in gold bullion from Great Britain's South African gold mines.

The importance of London's control of South African gold mines is directly related to the drug trade in the Orient.

Gold is the only medium of monetary exchange accepted by opium farmers. British bankers at Hong Kong pay the Chinese mad Societies in gold bullion for their heroin. The gold is then used to purchase raw opium from the farmers. From the farmers the opium is transported by mule train to the drug manufacturers. The cycle is complete when the heroin is shipped to Hong Kong in exchange for more gold.

An ever-increasing demand for gold, therefore, was directly proportionate to the escalating drug market. British Masonic bankers knew that their South African gold mines could not provide an endless supply, but central banking could—so long as central banking in every nation was under their control. How English Freemasonry accomplished this feat will be discussed in chapters 4 and 5.

Meanwhile, within four years after the end of the Second Opium War, Great Britain held financial control of seven-eighths of the vastly expanding opium trade into China. This trade amounted to over $20 million in 1864 alone.

Over the next twenty years, the total opium exported from India most of which went to China—skyrocketed from 58,681 chests in 1860, to 105,508 chests in 1880. Although the Manchu dynasty still opposed the trade, by 1898 China was well established in growing its own poppy for export. The controllers of the growing, manufacturing, and distribution of the drugs were the Chinese Triads, the financiers of the Chinese Republicans.

With drug revenue to finance the overthrow of the dynasty, the Chinese Republicans deposed the Manchus on February 15, 1912. Leading the rebellion was the westernized triad enforcement officer Dr. Sun Yat Sem, Dr. Sen's successor was General Chiang Kai-shek, himself a member of the old style mad Society. Alfred W. McCoy in his monumental study, The politics of heroin in South-East Asia, shares the evaluation of a Chinese historian of these events: "Perhaps for the first time in Chinese history, the underworld gained formal recognition in national politics." Fenton Bresler, in his book The Chinese Mafia, informs us that

> "the Triads became the strong-arm of Chiang Kai-shek's rule: generals, soldiers, intelligence workers, villains, gangsters, drug traffickers, businessmen, murderers, a mixture of the honest and the criminal."

At the center of the Chinese revolution was Hong Kong. British Freemasonry had foreseen that the triad-backed Republicans would sooner or later overthrow the Manchus. In 1898, a decade before the revolution, London signed a ninety-nine year lease with the Chinese for the "free port" of Hong Kong. The sole purpose of the lease was to establish "offshore" banking that would be exempt from Chinese audits, no matter what government was in power. To this day no Hong Kong bank has been audited by any Chinese government, nor has any outgoing ship been checked for cargoes of opium.

From this beginning at Hong Kong in 1898 the offshore banking of British Freemasonry was destined to spread around the world. In fact, Fenton Bresler informs us that illegal drugs are today transported to the West on Royal British Fleet Auxiliary vessels which supply the Royal Navy all over the world. Bresler also documents throughout his book how the ruthless mafia-style Triads continue to protect their British Masonic lords.

By the beginning of the twentieth century, the narcotics problem had become universal and severe. In response, an international conference was held at The Hague in 1911 (where England had founded one of her first Masonic Lodges on the Continent in 1731). This gathering became known as the "Hague Convention," which itself was a follow-up to an Anglo-Chinese agreement made in 1905. World pressure on England and China had forced an agreement to curtail drug traffic; the Chinese agreed "to reduce domestic opium production, while the British were to reduce their exports to China from British India correspondingly."

The purpose of The Hague Convention was to regulate the narcotics trade, with the goal of eventual total suppression. The success of The Hague Convention depended on strict enforcement of the earlier Anglo-Chinese agreement of 1905. The British, however, completely evaded both the 1905 and 1911 agreements by shipping opium to their unregulated extraterritorial bases, Hong Kong and Shanghai. The Chinese, who had subscribed enthusiastically to both protocols, soon discovered that the number of licensed opium dens in the Shanghai International Settlement had jumped from eighty-seven in 1911 at the time of The Hague Convention to 663 in 1914. In addition, the Triads, backed by British Masonry and operating out of the warehouses of Shanghai, doubled their smuggling operations to inland China.

The British Masonic drug lords had remembered well the treaty that followed the First Opium War, which created a massive bookkeeping burden to handle import duties. They would tolerate no repetition of that with the Hague Convention. The end result was that the Hague Convention failed to regulate the narcotics trade. Instead, Masonic drug traffickers sidestepped its protocols by moving production and distribution to the black market. Predictably, profits increased.

The broad compatibility between British Masonic banking and the worldwide production of drugs can be seen from the following and telling example. In 1911, London issued a major new loan to Persia (now Iran), the collateral of which was Persia's opium revenues. This kind of international loan became the new way by which the British Masonic Oligarchy could legally and vastly increase its wealth. By advancing money to Third World nations, the Masonic financiers can in effect say, we're only loaning money to this nation. We can't help how it's repaid.

China: from Democracy to Communism

The wealth of any nation today is determined by its trade with other nations. If a nation sells less than it buys in return, it is said to have a trade deficit. If it sells more, it has a trade surplus, which results in an increase of its gold supply. For example, the two world wars made the United States of America the wealthiest nation on earth because it's industrial output to supply war materials to allied nations was far greater than what it purchased abroad. By the end of World War Il, America held in reserve most of the world's gold.

Each nation in the world struggles to develop something unique to sell to other nations: banking services, oil, agricultural products, steel, gold, diamonds, computer technology, and narcotics. Terms, such as banking economy, oil economy, agricultural economy, industrial economy, or narco-economy define any given nation's economic output. If a nation sells more of its economic output than it buys, it becomes wealthy. How that wealth is distributed to its citizens will determine whether a middle-class will develop. Absolute monarchies, communist republics, socialist republics, and corrupt democratic republics generally have no middle class, because the rich and powerful control a strong central government, thereby keeping most of the citizenry poor. On the other hand, constitutional monarchies and democratic republics that protect citizens with a "bill of rights" and assure a free enterprise system with protective laws and tax incentives, spread their wealth more evenly among its citizens, thus developing a strong middle class.

By nature, nations with narco-backed economies are corrupt. Not only are their citizens poor, the corrupt narco-rich, who fund their own private army to dispose of enemies, bribe corrupt politicians so they can operate with impunity. Such was the China ruled by Triad member, Chiang Kai-shek. Although the British Masonic Hong Kong banks supported Chiang with narco-dollars, he faced opposition to his ambitions to head a free, republican China.

To the north Grand Orient Freemason Mao Tse Tung, commander of the Chinese Red Army, had in the fall of 1926 captured the northern seaport of Shanghai, by then the country's largest and most modern city. The recapture of Shanghai was essential to Chiang Kai-shek and his narco-funded republican party. Chiang, therefore, solicited the help of the Triad Society in Shanghai, known as the Green Pang and which was headed by a brilliant young villain named Tu Yueh Sheng.

The Triads were the strong-arm wing of Chiang's republican party, which was known as the Chinese Nationalist Party, or Kuomintang (KMT). Chiang used the Triads for jobs his official KMT army could not do. For example, in the spring of 1927, soon after he arrived in Shanghai, Chiang met with Tu secretly to plan the destruction of the Communists. The morning of April 12, 1927, Green Pang thugs massacred almost all the members of the

Communist-led labor unions. As a reward, Tu received the official rank of major-general in the KMT Army and was unofficially "allowed to consolidate his position as the 'Opium King' of Chiang Kai-shek's China".

Mao Tse-Tung, however, had plans of his own. If drug revenues could finance the free society of China, it could also bankroll Communism. In 1928 the Chinese Red Army began planting large fields of poppy in areas over which they had won control." British Freemasonry, not opposed doing business with anyone who grew poppy, bought opium from Mao through its Hong Kong banks. By 1935 the Communists more opium fields than did the Republic.

Chiang Kai-shek's revenues began to decline and his political days were numbered.

After World War Il, China in effect was handed over to the Communists by the West by the decision to refuse General Chiang Kai-shek military help. In 1949, remnants of the general's rag-tag KMT army fled to opium-rich Burma, where it built airstrips to fly opium to South Vietnam. Some Triad Societies went with them, while others fled to Hong Kong. The Communists, now in control of mainland China, sought throughout the 1950s to extend their territory by supporting Ho Chi Minh, president of North Vietnam from 1945 to 1969, while constantly fighting the remnants of the KMT for control of drug trade in the Golden Triangle. The Golden Triangle is comprised of the rugged Shan hills of northeastern Burma, the mountain ridges of northern Thailand, and the Meo highlands of northern Laos. In the 1960s, these skirmishes, which by then had involved North Vietnam, erupted into a full-blown war, known as the Vietnam War, a drug war which will be discussed in chapter 8.

Meanwhile, needing the financial support of the Hong Kong banks to back his own narco-economy, Mao Tse Tung permitted the British lease of Hong Kong to continue. The British bankers carried on business as usual. By 1983, Red China had nine million acres of poppy under cultivation. Today sixty-four percent of the

Peking government's income comes from the drug trade, while fifty to seventy percent of the world's drugs are refined in 101 legal narcotics factories in mainland China.

More Wars Bring More Drugs

Meanwhile, as a welcomed relief for the battlefield wounded, the purchase of narcotics during World War I brought more wealth to the Masonic drug barons. After the war the vast warehouses of opium needed new customers. The new market was Japan. So widely known was this British traffic into Japan that even the U.S. weekly magazine, The Nation, ran a series of documentary reports highly critical of the British role in illegal drugs.

By this time the League of Nations had been founded by Grand Orient Freemasonry, the bitter enemy of English Freemasonry. The League of Nations Opium Committee demanded that the British government account for the vast discrepancies between the official figures on opium shipments into Japan released respectively by the Japanese and British governments. From 1916 to 1920, Japanese figures showed a thriving British traffic; London claimed only negligible shipments, all earmarked for medical use. When confronted with this discrepancy as prima facie evidence of large-scale British black market smuggling of opium into Japan, the British delegate argued that such black-marketeering merely proved the case for creating a government-owned opium monopoly.

London had little concern for the views of the League of Nations. For example, in 1923, after a British government commission under Lord Inchcape had investigated India's finances, its report went on to warn against reducing the acres of poppy under cultivation, because of the need to safeguard "this most important source of revenue."

Inchcape was a direct descendant of the Masonic founder of the Peninsular & Orient Steamship Line which transported drugs a century earlier. As heir to the family's fortune, he had good reason to endorse continued opium production in British India. Brian Ingles wrote in *The Forbidden Game: A Social History of Drugs* (1975) that

> "while the British Government was professing to be taking measures to reduce consumption of opium and hemp drugs, its agents in India were in fact busy pushing sales in order to increase the colony's revenues."

By 1923 the United States Congress was concerned about the British-run black market in opium. Representative Stephen Porter, Chairman of the U.S. House of Representatives Foreign Affairs Committee, introduced and passed a bill through Congress that called for country-by-country production and import quotas on opium, with the goal of reducing consumption by ninety percent. The ten percent left represented generally accepted levels of necessary medical consumption.

Porter's proposal was brought before the League of Nations Opium Committee, where it was publicly opposed by the British representative. In defiance of the world community, the British delegate drafted an amendment to Porter's plan which called for increased quotas to account for "legitimate opium consumption" beyond medical use. The quotas assigned beyond that required for medical use referred, of course, to the opium needed to supply the massive addict population in British colonies and spheres of influence where opium was unregulated. The U.S. and Chinese delegations were enraged and led a walkout of the Plenipotentiary session, while the British rubber-stamped the creation Of a Central Narcotics Board, which was designated with authority to gather information and nothing more. Journalists stationed in Geneva henceforth referred to what remained of the Committee as the "Smugglers Reunion."

The attempt by the League of Nations to regulate the escalating illegal drug traffic controlled by the British was met with such shenanigans at every turn. How was it that London was able to rebuff every political attempt to thwart her trafficking in narcotics? The answer can be found in her control of the political machines and financial institutions of all industrial nations. The next chapter will document how English Freemasonry took over politics of the world's seven largest industrial nations to that her number one income producer—narcotics—would always be secure.

Chapter 3

English Freemasonry Secret Agenda for Political Control of America

(The day) I (became) a member in the Masonic order, I (saw) the wealth and power they possess, the influence they hold. I think over their ceremonies and I wonder (how) a large body of men can devote themselves to what at times appear the most ridiculous and absurd rites without an object and without an end.

Why should we not form a secret society with but one object— the furtherance of the British Empire and the bringing of the whole uncivilized world under British rule, for the recovery of the United States, [and] for ... making the Anglo-Saxon race but one Empire?

Cecil Rhodes

The once powerful British Empire, on which the sun never set, was on the wane following the loss of its American colonies. Anything said about world government emanated from Paris, not London. Throughout most of the nineteenth century, French Freemasonry, and not English Freemasonry, appeared to be the dominant revolutionary force in the Old World—offering the lower and middle classes a voice in government. English Freemasonry was partially to blame for the decline of the British empire. Since its beginning in 1717, the British Brotherhood was aristocratic, capitalistic, and monopolistic. Prior to the Victorian era of the nineteenth century, upper-class income came from ground rent, banking and trade. A middle class hardly existed in England in those days. The uneducated lower class had little chance of economic or social improvement.

The right-wing aristocracy of Great Britain, who were wrapped up in English Freemasonry, were called "British race patriots" by their Grand Orient left-wing opponents. British race patriots believed that the British race was at a higher evolutionary level than other races. When French Grand Orient Freemasonry sent a German-born Mason, Karl Marx (1818, 1883), to England to agitate the lower classes to rebel against the aristocracy, the British race patriots at least became concerned about the political to ascendancy which French Freemasonry had enjoyed for the last hundred years. To counter the increasingly influential ideology of French Freemasonry, in 1870 a select group of English Masons devised a plan which would both satisfy the proletariat and keep the Masonic oligarchy in power. The scheme was introduced at Christ Church, Oxford, by Freemason John Ruskin.

John Ruskin (1819–1900), writer, critic, artist, and British race patriot, was born of wealthy but strict parents.

Ruskin had received his formal education at Christ Church College, Oxford University. A course on Plato's Republic had been his favorite. Ruskin's inspiration and devotion to the creation of an elite of race patriots derived directly from Plato's Republic, which he read almost daily. In the Republic, Plato called for "a ruling class with a powerful army to keep it in power and a society completely subordinate to the monolithic authority of the rulers." Ruskin's studies of ancient political philosophers taught him that the most effective way to conquer a man is to capture his mind. Realizing that a century earlier French Masons had captured the working man's mind through revolutionary propaganda, Ruskin set out to recoup a extend the influence of British Masonry. He wanted to do this by the education of the working man.

In 1870, Ruskin was asked to return to Oxford to hold a chair in the fine arts. His inaugural lecture, which set forth his views on the ruling class as developed from Plato's Republic, sent shock waves through Oxford. The undergraduates to whom Ruskin spoke were the scions of the British aristocracy. They listened with awe at Ruskin's message, of which a portion follows:

> (You, the undergraduates are) the possessors of a magnificent tradition of education, beauty, rule of law, freedom, decency, and self-discipline but ... this tradition [can] not be saved, and [does] not deserve to be saved, unless it (can) be extended to the lower classes in England itself and to the non-English masses throughout the world. If this precious tradition (is) not extended to these two great majorities, the minority of upper-class Englishmen [will] ultimately be submerged by these majorities and the tradition lost. To prevent this, the tradition must be extended to the masses and to the empire [emphasis added].

Historians have touted Ruskin as a protector and educator of the downtrodden masses of the working men and the poor. In reality he had another rationale for proclaiming such ideas. He planted in the fertile minds of his Oxford students the theory that if they educated the working man and elevated him to the middle class, he would then labor in behalf of the aristocracy to perpetuate the tradition of the upper-class Englishmen which tradition was to control the finances of nations through ground rent, banking and trade. Ruskin taught that it was the essential duty of the aristocracy to guarantee an education for the poor not at the expense of the aristocracy, but so that an expanded middle class would, to all appearances, rule the country. This arrangement would be a type of legal slavery whereby both classes would benefit. Through the power of finance, the ruling class would maintain control from behind the scenes, while the working class would have opportunity to share in the common wealth made available through loans.

Ruskin successfully transmitted this vision to his students at Oxford. They in turn became the Masonic movers and shakers in the new politics and economics that today govern the seven industrial nations of the world—the United States, Canada, England, Germany, France, Italy, and Japan. The six key men in

Ruskin's audience of undergraduates were Arnold Toynbee, Arthur Glazebrook, George Parkin, Philip Lyttleton Gell, Henry Birchenough, and Alfred Milner. These men were so moved by Ruskin's speech that they devoted the rest of their lives to carrying out his ideals. The most famous of the group were Toynbee (1852–1883) and Milner (1854–1925).

Arnold Toynbee died prematurely in 1883, and in his honor the remaining five, along with Samuel Barnett, built Toynbee Hall in 1884 in London's East End slums as a model for government housing projects and welfare programs, and it remains so to this day. Alfred Milner, who is the most famous of the six disciples of Ruskin, coined the phrase "British race patriot." More on Milner later in this chapter.

Freemason Cecil Rhodes

A wealthy young man by the name of Cecil Rhodes (1853–1902) had begun his eight-year college career at Oxford in 1873, just three years after Ruskin's speech. Upon reading Ruskin's allocution, Rhodes was so impressed that he copied it in longhand and kept it with him for the rest of his life. Like Ruskin, Rhodes believed that the British and their Empire were the blessings of Providence upon the earth and its inhabitants—that only the British elite could and should rule the world to the benefit and happiness of mankind. To that end Rhodes labored for the rest of his short life.

As a youth, Rhodes had been sent by his parents to join his brother in South Africa to mine for gold. He was already a wealthy man when he began his education at Oxford in 1873. Shortly after arriving on campus, Rhodes was initiated into Freemasonry at the Apollo University Lodge No. 357. On April 17, 1877, he was raised a Master Mason in the same lodge. Rhodes also joined a Scottish Rite Lodge at Oxford called Prince Rose Croix Lodge No. 30. Rhodes divided his life between his studies at Oxford and mining at Kimberley, South Africa, and eight years later, in 1881, he graduated. By this time Rhodes had built up enough collateral that with backing from the House of Rothschild he was able to finance the purchase of DeBeers Diamond Mining Company and Consolidated Gold Fields in South Africa. By 1890 he had become the British administrator and financier of South Africa.

DeBeers and Consolidated produced for Rhodes a present-day equivalent of $10 million in annual income. When Rhodes died in 1902 at age 48, he left a will—the third—which dictated that a trust of his disciples governs the gigantic fortune he left behind. He wrote seven famous wills, of which the two most remembered are his first, which funded a secret society he had outlined but not organized in his lifetime, and the last, which established an educational grant to the University of Oxford—the Rhodes Scholarship.

What sort of character was Cecil Rhodes? Rhodes was, in fact, a critic of English Freemasonry—of its impotence and incompetence in advancing British race interests. His wills, and a document he composed in 1877 while at Oxford, testify to this fact. After being raised to Master Mason on April 17, 1877, Rhodes drafted a three-step program for world dominion for the British race patriots. The first part of the program enunciated the racial assumptions of the ruling elite and voiced their lingering regret over the loss of the American colonies. Rhodes wrote:

If we had retained America, there would at this moment be millions more of English living. I contend that we are the finest race in the world and that the more of the world we inhabit the better it is for the human race. Just fancy those parts that are at present inhabited by the most despicable specimens of human beings. What an alteration there would be if they were brought under Anglo-Saxon influence. Look again at the extra employment a new country added to our dominions gives. I contend that every acre added to our territory means in the future birth to some more of the English race who otherwise would not be brought into existence.

The second step of Rhode's program outlined the imperial ambitions of the British race patriots, of whom Rhodes was clearly one. Rhodes explained,

"It is our duty to seize every opportunity of acquiring more territory. And we should keep this one idea steadily before our eyes—more territory simply means more of the Anglo-Saxon race, more of the best, the most human, most honourable race the world possesses."

The third step of the program set forth Rhodes's political goals for world peace. World rule would bring world peace. As Rhodes said,

"the absorption of the greater portion of the world under our rule simply means the end of all wars."

To guarantee the funding from his vast wealth of his World Vision for the British empire, Rhodes wrote in 1877 the first of seven famous wills that he composed over his lifetime. Each of the wills was discreet and legally binding, and none superseded any other. The first will called for the formation of a "secret society" whose primary function would be focused on returning England to her former glory. He viewed English Freemasonry and its conspiracy as impotent and in effect defunct in. this regard. Ironically, when the society Rhodes had envisioned was finally organized after his death, its membership consisted only of English Freemasons. "The Round Table," as it was known, soon became the most powerful appendage of the British Brotherhood.

Rhodes's new conspiracy would ultimately reach most of tr.: developing world, and recapture the United States.

In this first will Rhodes compares the ineptitude of English Freemasonry with his own scheme:

(The day) I [became] a member in the Masonic order, I (saw) the wealth and power they possess, the influence they hold. I think over their ceremonies and I wonder [how] a large body of men can devote themselves to what at times appear the most ridiculous and absurd rites without an object and without an end.

> Why should we not form a secret society with but one object—
> the furtherance of the British Empire and the bringing of the
> whole uncivilized world under British rule, for the recovery of
> the United States, (and) for … making the Anglo-Saxon race
> but one Empire?

Rhodes Scholarships

Cecil Rhodes's last will established an educational grant to the
University of Oxford——the Rhodes Scholarship.

The trustees of the scholarship, who select students for the
prestigious award, are all English Freemasons and members of
the secret society of which Rhodes dreamed. Adhering to the
racial beliefs and prejudices of Cecil Rhodes the Trustees were
originally highly selective and racist. Until 1976 the scholarship
was bestowed only on hand-picked white males with at least five
years' residency in the British Commonwealth or colonies the
Republic of South Africa, or the United States of America.

Recipients of the Rhodes Scholarships have never been required
to be Masons, but they are indirectly controlled by English
Freemasonry for the rest of their lives. As you recall, the control
mechanism was established by John Ruskin, who realized and
taught that the mind of the laborer could be shaped and directed
through education—not to elevate the laborer at the expense of
the aristocracy, but so that an expanded middle class would, to all
appearances, rule the country.

Rhodes Scholars study at Oxford under English Masonic
professors, who, for a century have been believers in, and
promoters of, the natural superiority of the British race. Not
surprisingly Rhodes Scholars become British race patriots. Upon
graduation they return to their respective counties to act out the
role for which they have been educated. Masons or not, as
Anglophiles favoring England and everything English, they
further the English Masonic conspiracy. Some become
professors. Others go into finance, politics, or become political
advisors. In America, in addition to their chosen vocation, they

become "fellows" in one or more of the Anglophile Masonic fronts, such as the Brookings Institute, the Council on Foreign Relations, or the Trilateral Commission. Hence, we see the importance of a Rhodes Scholar. His or her career is devoted to the furtherance of English Freemasonry's plan to rule the world with her elite.

Rhodes's Secret Society: The Round Table

In his third will Rhodes left his entire estate to Freemason Lord Nathan Rothschild as trustee. Rhodes stipulated that his gigantic fortune be used by his disciples to carry out the program he had envisioned. As trustee, Rothschild appointed Freemason Alfred Milner to head up the secret society for which Rhodes's first will made provision. Lord Milner was the ideal man for the job. He once remarked of himself:

> "I am a British nationalist. If I am also an imperialist, it is because the destiny of the English race ... has been to strike fresh roots in distant parts... My patriotism knows no geographical but only racial limits. I am an imperialist and not a Little Englander, because I am a British Race."

From 1897 to 1905, Milner was governor-general and high commissioner of South Africa. Upon his appointment by Rothschild to chair Rhodes's secret society, Milner recruited a group of young men from Oxford and Hall to assist him in organizing his administration of the new society. All were respected English Freemasons. Among them were Rudyard Kipling, Arthur Balfour, Lord Rothschild, and some Oxford College graduates known as "Milner's Kindergarten." In 1909, Milner's Kindergarten, with some other English Masons, founded the Round Table. The grandfather of all modern British Masonic "think tanks" was born.

Three powerful think tank offshoots of the Round Table are (1) the Royal Institute of International Affairs (RIIA), organized in 1919 in London; (2) the Council on Foreign Relations (CFR), organized in 1921 in New York City; and (3) the Institute of

Pacific Relations (IPR), organized in 1925 for the twelve countries holding territory in what today we call the Pacific Rim.

Subsequent events reveal that the initial assignment of the Round Table was not necessarily to destroy the political experiments of French Freemasonry, such as socialism and communism, but to cooperate with them for the advancement of the English Masonic conspiracy. For this reason the Round Table think tanks opened their membership to men with contrary political and economic opinions, men who were noted Marxists such as H.G. Wells (1866–1946) and John Maynard Keynes (1883–1946). Yet, without exception, all were English Freemasons.

Dr. Carroll Quigley in Tragedy and Hope (1966) notes the impact these men had upon the politics of their day:

> "Through (Milner's) influence these men were able to win influential posts in government and international finance and became the dominant influence in British imperial and foreign affairs..."

In 1902, the year Cecil Rhodes died, and some seven years before the Organization of the Round Table, of which H.G. Wells would be a founding member, Wells anticipated the future existence of these British Masonic think tanks in a work entitled Anticipations of the Reaction to Mechanical and Scient Progress upon Human Life and Thought. In this farsighted piece, Wells explained the strategy by which aristocratic English Freemasonry would reach its goal of world dominion. He called it an "Open Conspiracy" as opposed to French Freemasonry's closed, or secret conspiracy.

The Open Conspiracy will appear first, I believe, as a conscious organization of intelligent and quite possibly in some cases wealthy men, as a movement having distinct social and political aims, confessedly ignoring most of the existing apparatus of political control, or using it only as an incidental implement in the attainment of these aims. It will be very loosely organized in its earlier stages, a mere movement of a number of people in a certain direction, who will presently discover with a sort of surprise the common object toward which they are all moving...

A confluent system of Trust-owned business organizations and of Universities and reorganized military and naval services may presently discover an essential unity of purpose, presently begin thinking a literature, and behaving like a State—a sort of outspoken Secret Society—an informal and open freemasonry (sic). In all sorts of ways, they will be influencing and controlling the apparatus of the ostensible governments.

Wells was in fact describing the methods and purposes of what would be the Round Table. The activity of the Round Table, operating as "an informal and open freemasonry," closed the era of British colonialism and opened the new era of a Commonwealth of Nations. Under Lord Milner's direction, from 1909 to 1913, Round Table groups, as the appendages of the original group were referred to outside of Great Britain, were organized in the chief British dependencies and in the United States. The scheme included bringing the United States of America once again under the dominance of London. These Round Table groups still function in eight countries today, and keep in touch through their quarterly magazine, The Round Table.

While the Round Table is an Anglophile secret order, conspiracy researchers in America have described it as left-wing because of its anti American activity. Dr. Quigley explains: There does exist, and has existed for a generation, an international Anglophile network which operates, to some extent, in the way the radical Right believes the Communists act. In fact, this network, which we may identify as the Round Table Groups, has no aversion to cooperating with the Communists, or any other groups, and frequently does so.

According to carol White, in The New Dark Ages Conspiracy (1980)' the consensus of the British Round Table groups, even before the First World War was a reality, was two-fold. First, America's industrial military complex was to be utilized to fight

Great Britain's wars, pay its bills' and force London's policies on the rest of the world.

Second, Germany' France, and Russia were to be pitted against each other in conflicts that were expected to erupt into war.

The Round Table was more informally known as the Cliveden Set. Cliveden was the name of the powerful and influential Masonic Astor family's estate where the Round Table met. The Astors owned two London newspapers, the *Patt Malt Gazette* and the *London Times*. The Round Table and its think tank spin-offs were the first organizations to engage in crisis management. English Masons did not conspire to create crises to overthrow governments, as did French Grand Orient Masons. Instead, the Round Table operated according to the doctrine of gradualism. Instead of instigating the political and economic chaos that pervaded society prior to and after World War I, these organizations took a "wait and see" attitude. They attempted to shape and manage crises to the advantage of Great Britain.

Most of these conspirators were 33rd degree Masons. Their motto, emblazoned on their Supreme Council Jewel, is "Order out of Chaos." "Order" was their desire, "Chaos" their dilemma. After studying a problem and agreeing on a solution, they would then make themselves available to the seven industrial nations around the world as advisors. In turn, these governments seemed always to react positively to their suggestions.

JEWEL OF THE 33RD DEGREE

The British Masonic Capture of World Governance

In volume one, chapter 21 of *Scarlet and the Beast*, we learned that the League of Nations, established after World War I, was the creation Of French Freemasonry, and for the most part, Paris determined its direction. The League, however, was not intended to be the handmaiden of French Freemasonry alone. The Grand Orient made this clear several years later, when in 1923 at its annual convention, all Freemasonry was invited to participate in the League; in fact, all Masonry was urged to fulfill its "duty" to help in the creation of a unified Europe and ultimately of a world government:

> "It is the duty of universal Freemasonry to co-operate absolutely with the League of Nations in order that it may no longer have to Submit to the interested influences of Governments.
> The principal task of the League Nations ... (is) ... the creation of creation of a European spirit ... in brief, the formation of the United States of Europe, or rather World Federation."

Of course, the British race patriots of English Freemasonry were not at all happy with a United States of Europe that would eventually merge into a World Federation, for it was evident to them that Freemasonry intended to dictate policy determine in the League of Nations. The Round Table went into session to determinate, what could be done. The conclusion, as subsequent events reveal, was to usurp control of the League. This meant that both the British and American governments would have to participate in this world government body. England's cooperation was certain, but the United States Congress had read the Versailles Treaty and wanted nothing to do with the League. Yet it was imperative that the Americans cooperate if English Freemasonry was to be successful in a coup. The consensus of the 1918 Round Table meeting, therefore, was to send a delegation to the 1919 Paris Peace Conference in Versailles, and while there, meet with the American members of the Round Table to see how best to change the attitudes of the American people, not so much to save the League, but to guarantee that the American people would fully cooperate with the next World Government—a World Government that English Freemasonry intended to control.

After the Peace Conference: New Round Tables

The Round Table made its appearance at the Paris Peace Conference for the purpose of organizing a takeover of the League of Nations. The Round Table conspiracy involved a few Americans summoned to the Peace Conference—Americans who were willing to betray their own country for prestige and money. They were 33rd degree Grand Lodge Mason "Colonel" Edward Mandell House, 33rd degree Scottish Rite Mason Christian Herter, the Dulles brothers, John and Allen, and Walter Lippmann.

On May 19, 1919, just twelve days after the final draft of the Treaty of Versailles had been distributed and condemned by the world, Colonel House led his coterie of Americans to the Majestic Hotel in Paris to meet with members of the English Round Table "in order to form organization whose job it would be to propagandize the citizens of America, England and Western Europe on the glories of World Government." This secret meeting resolved to expand the Round Table, not only in England, but in America and the Far East, by creating additional societies influence foreign policy in those various arenas.

The organizational structures of three political think tanks that would influence the politics of London, Washington and Tokyo were drawn up at the Paris Majestic Hotel meeting. The purpose of these groups, of course, was and is to develop an international consensus in the project to create World Government with the cooperation of all three Masonic obediences American, English and French.

Returning to London immediately after the Paris Peace Conference, the British Round Table met again at Cliveden, the estate of the Masonic Astor family, to implement their plans. The front organization which the British Round Table had already established to influence the foreign policy of Great Britain was the Royal Institute of International Affairs (RIIA). The chief financial supporter of the RITA was the Astor family. In the Far East, the Institute of Pacific Relations (IPR) was established. The machinations of the IPR would eventually involve America in a ten-year drug war in Vietnam for English Freemasonry a war never intended to be won militarily.

Colonel House took the plans for the Council on Foreign Relations (CFR) back to New York where he completed its charter. All the key members of the CFR were and are Scottish Rite Freemasons. However, it also admits members from other Masonic affiliations, as well as from all secret and metaphysical societies. On July 29, 1921, the following Masons were present at the founding meeting of the Council on Foreign Relations: 33rd degree English Grand Lodge Mason "Colonel" Edward Mandell House (1858–1938), personal advisor to President Woodrow Wilson; 33rd degree Scottish Rite Mason Christian Herter (1895–1966), later to be appointed Secretary of State under Eisenhower after John Foster Dulles's death; two 33rd degree Grand Orient Masons. Paul Warburg (1868–1932) and Jacob Schiff (1847–1921), both German born bankers sent to America to establish a central bank; Scottish Rite Mason Averell Harriman (1891-), whose family built the railroads of America; and 33rd degree Scottish Rite Mason Bernard Baruch (IS701965), an American Jewish banker and investor in silver. Other important founding members with no record of being Masons were Walter Lippmann (1889–1974), who would become one of the liberal establishment's favorite syndicated columnists and a contributing journalist to The New Republic the Anglophile magazine in America named after the Round Table's design for recapturing the United States; John Foster Dulles (1888–1959), later to serve as Secretary of State under President Eisenhower; Allen Dulles (1893–1969), John's brother who was destined to become director of the CIA in 1953; the banker J.P. Morgan, Jr. (1867–1943), son of the Civil War banker J.P. Morgan, sr. (1837–1913); and the banker and oilman John D. Rockefeller (18,391,937). When Rockefeller's sons came of age, they too joined the CFR.

The most famous of the brothers, and the most successful financially, is David Rockefeller (1915–2017), a major stockholder in the Exxon Oil Company and the Chase Manhattan Bank. In 1973, David Rockefeller founded the CFR spin-off—the Trilateral Commission (TC).

The CFR immediately began the long-range process of replacing pro-American politicians with Anglophile politicians. From the 1920s through World War Il, pro-America Masons held key positions in our government. For example, in 1923, 69 percent of congressmen and 63 percent of senators were Masons. By 1948 that percentage had dropped to 54 and 53 respectively. By 1984 the percentages had fallen to 12 and 14 percent respectively.

What is not normally realized is the fact that many government positions, once staffed by pro-America Masons, are now filled by persons who are members of the pro-British Masonic front, the Council on Foreign Relations.

For example, in the 1920s and 1930s, many young and aspiring politicians were "appointed" to the CFR, where they were educated on the merits of Anglophile internationalism. Likewise, young American intellectuals selected for the Rhodes Scholarship and educated at Oxford, were sent back to the United States, where they entered political life. These students of the CFR came of age in 1939 when they began filling posts in our federal government. By 1945 the State Department had, in effect, been completely taken over by the Council on Foreign Relations. How influential has the council on Foreign Relations been? Since its founding, and continuing through the Clinton administration, seventeen of twenty-three secretaries of the treasury have been members of the CFR.

Another seventeen of twenty-one secretaries of state have been members. Since 1944, all presidential candidates, both Republican and Democrat, have either been members of the CFR or its 1973 offshoot, the Trilateral Commission. The only exception was Harry Truman, who though a 33rd degree Mason, was not voted into office.

Six of the seven superintendents of West Point, every Supreme Allied Commander in Europe, and every U.S. ambassador to N.A.T.O. has been a member of the CFR.

British World Governance and the United Nations

After World War I, French Grand Orient Freemasonry considered itself mistress of the future. Grand Orient Masons were in charge of the new European politics from 1918 to 1930. They promised the world an era of peace, happiness, and prosperity through their Grand Orient children socialism and communism. Instead, Europe was plunged into revolution followed by counterrevolution, proponents of English and French Freemasonry.

Traditional monarchies, under the aegis of English Freemasonry, were destroyed in favor of French Freemasonry's socialist and communist republics. Left-wing dictators—more despotic than former sovereigns had ever been—ruled the new republics. Grand Orient republics, whether communist or socialist, became instruments for terror and disruption of order. French Freemasonry showed that, when in power, it was incapable of governing and maintaining order. General chaos and financial breakdown followed—ending in the Great Depression of the 1930s.

In Germany, Austria, Hungary and Italy, communism was eventually strangled at great cost and much bloodshed.

In place of communism, authoritarian regimes sprang up by popular consent. Such were the dictatorships of Admiral Horthy in Hungary, of Mussolini's fascism in Italy, of Chancellor Dollfuss in Austria, and Hitler's National Socialism in Germany.

By 1939, the French Grand Orient, which had once envisioned itself mistress of the future, found it had fallen on hard times. As one critic and chronicler of French Masonry Leon de Poncins wrote:

"The results were disastrous. The Treaty of Versailles quickly led to widespread breakdown of order, to revolutionary unrest, to the opposing reactions of the Fascist and Hitler regimes, to the Spanish Civil War, and finally to the Second World War."

English Freemasonry, which had been patiently implementing its policy of "gradualism" through the Round Table groups, saw its opportunity to regain dominance. She would accomplish this not by reinstating her kings throughout Europe, but by providing financial support for the extreme right-wing dictators who had wrested government from the hands of the extreme left-wing despots.

In 1939, the moment the round Table groups had been anticipating arrived. World War Il began and the League of Nations ceased operations. London's Round Table groups in America made their move, in effect, to take over world governance. That year the Council on Foreign Relations offered its services to the U.S. State Department.

By 1940 the State Department had created the Division of Special Research headed by CFR member Leo Pasbolsky.

The task of Pasbolsky and his CFR staff was to submit a plan outlining an organization that would replace the League of Nations: they called their international body the United Nations. At least forty-seven members of the CFR were in the delegation that attended the U.N. Conference in San Francisco in 1945. And CFR members occupied nearly every significant decision-making post at the conference.

The stage was now set for America's entrance into this world body. Sympathy and receptivity toward the creation or such an institution had been cultivated in the House and Senate by a significant number of congressmen and senators who had become members of the CFR. When it was time to vote upon American entry into the United Nations, the majority voted in favor. The Rockefeller Foundation donated the land upon which the United Nations building would be built. Not surprisingly, at the time

David Rockefeller was chairman of the Council on Foreign Relations.

By founding the United Nations, English Freemasonry effectively wrested control of world government from French Freemasonry. As for America, the freedom from English rule that we won by our War of Independence in 1776, we returned to England with the creation of the Council on Foreign Relations. With the United Nations planted on our soil, the powerful might of our military would be co-opted. As the British Round Table had planned in 1909, the United States would fight Great Britain's wars and pay her bills. The former was accomplished by coming to the aid of Great Britain in two world wars. The latter was accomplished by the British Masonic takeover of our banking system, which will be discussed in the next chapter.

By founding the United Nations, English Freemasonry effectively wrested control of world government from French Freemasonry. As for America, the freedom from English rule that we won by our War of Independence in 1776, we returned to England with the creation of the Council on Foreign Relations. With the United Nations planted on our soil, the powerful might of our military would be co-opted. As the British Round Table had planned in 1909, the United States would fight Great Britain's wars and pay her bills. The former was accomplished by coming to the aid of Great Britain in two world wars. The latter was accomplished by the British Masonic takeover of our banking system, which will be discussed in the next chapter.

Chapter 4

FREEMASONRY AND CENTRAL BANKING

The money power preys upon the nation in times of peace and conspires against it in times of adversity. It is more despotic than monarchy, more insolent than autocracy, more selfish than bureaucracy. I see in the near future a crisis approaching that unnerves me, and causes me to tremble for the safety of my country. Corporations have been enthroned, an era of corruption will follow, and the money power of the country will endeavor to prolong its reign by working upon the prejudices of the people, until the wealth is aggregated in a few hands, and the republic is destroyed.

President Abraham Lincoln—1863

What Is Money?

Anything can serve as money that is acceptable to the general population as a medium of exchange—from the wampum beads of shells made by the American Indians to the brightly colored shells called cowries in India, to whales' teeth among the Figians, to coca leaves (cocaine) among the sixteenth century Incas, to tobacco among early colonists in North America, to large stone disks on the Pacific island of Yap, and to cigarettes and liquor after World War Il in Germany.

The most popular materials used for monetary exchange are gold and silver. The use of these metals began around the seventh century B.C. and continued through the next two and a half millenniums. In late eighteenth century Europe, paper money convertible to gold and silver became the most acceptable medium of exchange. The bearer of the note was guaranteed that at any time he could go to a local money exchange and his note would be redeemed for the specified amount of gold or silver printed thereon. This system demanded that the total value of paper money in circulation could not exceed the total amount of gold on deposit, which restricted the growth of the money supply. Therefore, during war when extra money was needed to build an army and supply war materials, governments were forced temporarily to go off the gold standard. In other words, during war paper money could not be converted to gold and a government printed instead an unlimited supply of "fiat money" to finance the war. Just as Webster defines fiat as "an authoritative or arbitrary order," so fiat money is "paper currency not convertible into gold or silver" by an "arbitrary order" of government. During a war paper money continued to be "legal tender," but could not be exchanged for gold or silver.

Fiat money was only as stable as the government that issued it. So long as adequate gold reserves existed, as well as a thriving economy, fiat money remained stable, even in time of war.

If the nation won the war, the government would simply reinstate a gold-convertible currency, and usually the transition went smoothly. If the nation lost the war, such as Germany after World War I, the paper money became worthless.

For these reasons, throughout the period of the European revolutions, from 1789 through World War I, we find governments going on and off gold-convertible paper money. After World War I, European nations went back on the gold standard, but the return to a gold-backed currency was short-lived because of the Great Depression of the 1930s. Since then, governments have permanently gone off the gold-convertible currency, printing instead "fiat money".

The Rise of the House of Rothschild

Our current standard of permanent fiat money began to develop after the French Revolution.

The horrors of the Reign of Terror that followed the revolution, and the subsequent Napoleonic Wars that engulfed the Continent from 1804–1815, struck terror in the hearts of the crowned heads of Europe. Foreseeing the danger to their thrones, the kings hired Meyer Amschel Rothschild (1744–1812), a Jewish financial wizard from Frankfurt, Germany, to transport their gold to safe havens.

Meyer Rothschild's financial success was in part fostered by the princely family of Thurn und Taxis, a family of Milanese extraction living in Frankfurt, Germany, and in part by his connections in the Masonic Lodge. Toward the end of the nineteenth century, the Thurn und Taxis had conceived a plan for a postal system in Central Europe. Some three centuries before, in 1516, the family had been commissioned by Emperor Maximilian I to inaugurate a mounted postal service between Vienna and Brussels. From then on the dignified rank of postmaster general was conferred on one of the members of the Thurn und Taxis family. At the turn of the nineteenth century, this important position was held by prince Karl Anselm. The prince, whose family had maintained an impeccable record of confidential handling of the mails for three hundred years, began opening mail before sending it on to its destination. He turned this practice to profit, and his biggest customer was Meyer Rothschild.

Meyer Rothschild had come to realize that it was of paramount importance to an investment banker to have at his disposal early and accurate information of important events, especially in time of war. As Prince Karl fed Rothschild "inside" information, Rothschild transacted several successful financial investments to the great satisfaction of the prince. While not illegal at the time, but certainly unethical, the practice of "insider trading" was born.

As a result of his success with the prince's finances, Meyer Rothschild was introduced to the last of the Holy Roman-German Emperors, Francis II. On January 29, 1800, Rothschild was granted the title of Imperial Crown Agent, which meant that for the first time in history a private banking house was in control of the realm's finances. The concept of central banking was born. That a central bank presents peril to sovereign nations is revealed in the following remark made by Meyer Rothschild:

> "Permit me to control the money of a nation, and I care not who makes its laws."

To provide better service to his royal patrons, Rothschild strategically located his five sons throughout Europe. His eldest son Amschel (17,731,885), headed the Frankfurt bank; Solomon (1774–1855) the Vienna bank; Nathan (1777–1836) the London bank; Carl (1788–1855) the Naples Bank; and James (1792–1868), the youngest son, headed the Paris bank when he came of age. Each son established central banking in his resident nation, making loans to the various governments at discount interest rates.

Freemasonry, Banking, and Insider Trading

Although Meyer Rothschild himself never became a Freemason to further his financial empire, his sons did, as did his head clerk, Sigmund Geisenheimer. Rabbi Marvin Antelman in *To Eliminate the Opiate* (1974) reports that Geisenheimer had wide-ranging Masonic contacts that crisscrossed Europe:

The Rothschilds utilized the services of Sigmund Geisenheimer, their head clerk, who in turn was aided by Itzig of Berlin, the Illuminati of the Toleraz Lodge and the Parisian Grand Orient Lodge. Geisenheirnrer was a member of the Mayence Masonic Illuminati Lodge, and was the founder of the Frankfurt Judenloge... At a later date the Rothschilds joined the Lodge. Solomon Meyer Rothschild (1774-18.55) was a member for a short while before moving to Vienna.

Since the days of Meyer Rothschild, international banking and the Masonic oligarchy have been inseparable, cooperating in their ever-expanding financial control of nation. Most citizens erroneously believe that the central banks in their respective nations are owned by their governments. Gary Allen, in *None Dare Call It Conspiracy*, rejects this misconception, stating that private monopolies hold central banks not governments:

Eventually these international bankers actually owned as private corporations the central banks of the various European nations. The Bank of England, Bank of France and Bank of Germany were not owned by their respective governments, as almost everyone imagines, but were privately owned monopolies granted by the heads of state, usually in return for loans.

The practice of private Masonic monopolies making loans to the British government is not new.

You recall that the British East India Company (BEIC) was granted a merchant shipping monopoly in 1657 by Oliver Cromwell in exchange for loans. These "merchants of the earth," all born and bred in English Freemasonry, literally carried the British flag around the world. Their descendants cooperated with Meyer Rothschild's son Nathan during the Napoleonic Wars to supply the kings of Europe with funds, war materials, and opium, all of which were smuggled from port to destination through a chain of English grand lodges.

The practice of private Masonic monopolies making loans to the British government is not new.

You recall that the British East India Company (BEIC) was granted a merchant shipping monopoly in 1657 by Oliver Cromwell in exchange for loans. These "merchants of the earth," all born and bred in English Freemasonry, literally carried the British flag around the world. Their descendants cooperated with Meyer Rothschild's son Nathan during the Napoleonic Wars to supply the kings of Europe with funds, war materials, and opium, all of which were smuggled from port to destination through a chain of English grand lodges.

Nathan and his brother James were the most successful of the Rothschild sons, and their success is in part attributable to their membership in the lodge. For instance, when James arrived in Paris to begin his career, he immediately joined French Grand Lodge Freemasonry, quickly rising to the 33rd degree of the Ancient and Accepted Scottish Rite of the French Supreme Council. Later we shall learn of the significance of James attending six Parisian Masonic festivals between 1841–1845.

Nathan, the most financially adept son, upheld the tradition of insider trading established by his father by joining the Lodge of Emulation in London on October 4, 1802. Not only did the lodge promote Nathan's smuggling operation to service the continental armies of his royal English patrons during Napoleon's Continental blockade, it is also suspected that the lodge assisted him in his bid to control the Bank of England. In June of 1815, the London stock market crashed because of an "erroneous" report issued by a government agent that Napoleon was winning the battle at Waterloo. Prices on the London Stock Exchange plummeted and Nathan bought up all the stock. The next day, when the report was proven false, and the following day when knowledge of Napoleon's defeat reached the street, the stock market rebounded and stocks went to unprecedented heights. Nathan unloaded his stocks, depositing his enormous profits in the Bank of England. Overnight Nathan controlled Great Britain's central bank.

Because of Nathan Rothschild's financial acumen, London became the banking headquarters of the house of Rothschild. All male descendants of this Jewish clan have since been attached to Gentile English Freemasonry, for no exclusively Jewish lodges exist in England. And to this day no Englishman has ever worked for N.M. Rothschild and Sons, at St. Swithin's Lane, unless first proving his ability to keep secrets by joining English Freemasonry. According to British investigative journalist Martin Short in *Inside The Brotherhood* (1989), unless you are a Mason, you do not work for London banks. The current managing director of the Rothschild bank, for example, is Freemason Michael Richardson, who for five years (1982–1987) was chairman of the board of the Royal Masonic Hospital.

Rothschild Wealth

Meyer Rothschild got his start in banking by charging European royalty commissions for transferring their gold to safe havens during the Napoleonic Wars. Rothschild shrewdly refused to accept fiat Money in payment of his commissions. Instead, he took an agreed upon percentage of the gold he was transporting. Before long he owned more gold than the kings he served. As the Napoleonic Wars dragged on, the monarchs depleted their wealth and then borrowed from Rothschild to continue their fight against the Corsican. The kings authorized Rothschild to issue fiat Money and then borrowed heavily from it. Of course, this system drove them deeper into debt, piling interest upon interest. To repay Rothschild they were forced to levy heavy taxes on their people.

Of the five Brothers, Nathan Rothschild reaped the most from this scheme. Just prior to Napoleon's defeat at Waterloo in 1815, the wealth of his bank in London stood at $3 million.

Five years later his holdings amounted to $7.5 billion. The increase was largely due to Nathan's profits from the London stock market crash in June, 1815. We cannot be sure of Nathan's net worth at the time of his death, but we can make a reasonable guess, bearing in mind that these are only estimates, since no inventory of the Rothschilds estates have ever been filed. In the house of Rothschild, because heirs do not inherit, there is no inheritance tax and therefore no requirement for estate inventory. In any case, it is unlikely that Nathan could have sustained over the next two decades the kind of growth that had occurred in 1815. It is reasonable to however, that he could have increased his wealth at the rate of ten percent annually, producing by the time of his death in 1836 an approximate $20 billion.

James Rothschild's endeavors also met with success. In 1848, the Paris house was estimated at 600 million francs as against 362 million francs for all the other Paris banks combined. When James died in 1868, the net worth of his bank in U.S. dollars was estimated at $200 million.

No records exist concerning the estimated wealth of the Berlin, Vienna and Naples branches of the Rothschild banking houses. They were strong enough, however, to dominate the money markets of those capitals as well. By the beginning of the 1900s, the wealth of the House of Rothschild had grown to such proportions that it was estimated that the Rothschilds controlled half the wealth on earth. During World War I, the British Rothschild family earned another $100 billion by loaning money to the warring nations. By 1925, their wealth was estimated at $300 billion. By 1940, that figure had increased to $500 billion—which then was about double all the wealth in the United States of America. And by figuring a modest five percent annual increase since 1940, we can estimate that the Rothschilds have accumulated to date well over $7 trillion which is almost twice what the United States has accumulated in debt during its two-hundred-year history. And to whom does Uncle Sam owe this debt? To the Masonic house of Rothschild and its affiliate central banks, which have financed our deficit spending spree since the end of World War II.

Centralizing Masonic Wealth in Switzerland

During Napoleon's first exile, the crowned heads of Europe called for the Congress of Vienna to plan a united strategy against the republicanization of Europe. In the course of nine months (September 1814 to June 1815), the map of Europe was redrawn. During this time Napoleon escaped from exile and raised another army, only to be defeated finally at Waterloo. With this second defeat of the French, Great Britain permanently severed the exclusive alliance French Freemasonry had with American Freemasonry. A new alliance, at least in respect to America, was formed between English Grand Lodge bankers and French Grand

Lodge bankers. Both cooperated in a century-long struggle to take over the banking system in America.

The strategy for this new Masonic alliance was contained within the final item on the agenda at the Congress of Vienna, which called for the protection of the wealth of royalty by making of Switzerland a bank with an army attached. Seagirt England, unhampered by the fears of landlocked Vienna, yet as determined to safeguard its own commercial and colonial interests abroad, was in full agreement to ratify Switzerland's neutrality. In Paris on November 20, 1815, Switzerland was guaranteed neutrality by France, Austria, Great Britain, Portugal, Prussia, Sweden, and Russia. Swiss borders since that date have remained stable.

London, however, did make one demand—Swiss Freemasonry must abandon its French obedience and adopt the constitution of English Freemasonry. From the beginning of the French Empire in 1804, Swiss lodges had been under the French Grand Orient constitution. To guarantee the protection of the financial interests of the Masonic oligarchy in England and on the Continent, English Freemasonry required the control of Swiss lodges for the purpose of intelligence gathering. Hence, shortly after the Congress of Vienna, London began a twenty-four year process of taking over fourteen of the fifteen Swiss lodges and recertifying them under English Grand Lodge obedience. Only one Grand Orient lodge was permitted to function, in Geneva, where many international conflicts have since been resolved. On July 22–24, 1844, the fourteen English-constituted Swiss grand lodges organized the Grand Lodge Alpina as their Swiss headquarters in Zurich, where the banking headquarters of the European and British Masonic oligarchy remains to this day.

With the Masonic oligarchy's wealth secure in Switzerland, an alliance between the central banks of the five Rothschild brothers in England and on the Continent was solidified. Mirroring their father's strategy, "Permit me to control the money of a nation, and I care not who makes its laws," the Rothschild brothers directed from behind the scenes the politics of Europe throughout the first half of nineteenth Century. Their attempt at taking over central banking in the United States during this period, however, was thwarted at every turn. By the time our Civil War had ended, the Rothschilds had become so suspect to Americans that the banking family was forced to act through the agency of other banking families. The House of Rothschild struck a deal with its German banking competitor, the house of Warburg, which set in motion a plan to establish central banking in America without the direct involvement of the Rothschild name. Not only were the Warburgs banking competitors, they were Masonic competitors as well. The Warburg Brothers, Max, Felix and Paul, were Grand Orient Masons. Nevertheless, Felix's Jacob Schiff, also a Grand Orient Mason, was sent to the United States after our Civil War to buy into the existing American banking firm of Kuhn, Loeb & Co. At Schiff's side was Paul Warburg.

Meanwhile, the British House of Rothschild funded J.P. Morgan and John D. Rockefeller to handle its banking interests in America. By 1913, with the passage of the Federal Reserve Act, the Rothschilds and the Warburgs were in complete control of our nation's money supply. This Act transferred the control of our money supply from Congress to the Federal Reserve Bank—a central bank not owned by our federal government, but owned by private stockholders who were European and British Masons bent on directing American politics for their own profit.

Proliferation of Central Banking

The purpose of a central bank in a nation is to stabilize the nation's economy by centralizing national credit within the nation. Congress controls fiscal policy and the government owns the majority of stock in the central bank, the central bank is operated to the benefit of the nation.

On the other hand, if the majority of stock is owned by private citizens, the central bank is operated to the benefit of those private stockholders.

By the time the Congress of Vienna had convened in the fall of 1814, the Rothschilds and their affiliate Masonic bankers had already established privately owned central banks throughout Europe. As Meyer Rothschild so aptly stated before he died, the real purpose of central banks in private hands is to increase the personal wealth of stockholders. It matters not who makes the laws.

In Europe, central banks were easy to establish for two reasons. First, the Rothschilds had only to negotiate with an absolute monarch. Second's the Napoleonic Wars forced the European monarchs to hire the House of Rothschild to protect their moveable wealth. When Meyer Rothschild became more wealthy than the monarchs, he would suggest that his banking firm be permitted to establish central banking in their kingdoms to stabilize the money supply.

Rothschild's suggestion would usually be granted by edict. In a democratic nation, such as the United States, it was not so simple, for Congress controlled both the fiscal policy and the money supply. Therefore, it took a century and the cooperation of both English and French Freemasonry before the House of Rothschild was able to take over the money supply of the United States.

With the defeat of the French at Waterloo in 1815, London was assured cooperation by Paris.

The plan called for both Freemasonries to participate in creating a civil war in America. Not only did this come to pass, but also the murder of three American presidents, the pay off of several key American congressmen, and the grooming of an American traitor for the presidency was required before the House of Rothschild finally succeeded in establishing the privately owned Federal Reserve Bank in 1913. Once this was accomplished, the Rothschilds were able legally to increase the wealth of the stockholders to the detriment of our nation.

The late Dr. Carroll Quigley, professor of history at Georgetown, Princeton, and Harvard universities, confirms in his book

Tragedy and Hope (1966) that central banks operate for the profit of the bankers and not for the good of the nation:

> The history of the last century shows ... that the advice given to governments by bankers ... was consistently good for bankers, but was often disastrous for governments, businessmen, and the people generally. Such advice could be enforced if necessary by manipulation of exchanges, gold flows, discount rates, and even levels of business activity.

The power of the banks to control the destinies of nations was leaked to the press after a stockholders meeting of the Midland Bank of London, England, in 1924. As all banks in London, the Midland Bank has its own Masonic lodge—the Holden Lodge No. 2946. The speaker at the podium of Midland's January 1924 stockholders' meeting was Freemason Reginald McKenna, Midland's chairman of the board and past chancellor Of the Exchequer of England from 1915 to 1916. His statement to the stockholders was and is testimony to the financial hold Masonic bankers have on governments to the detriment of the people:

> "I am afraid the ordinary citizen will not like to be told that the banks can, and do, create money... And they who control credit of the nation direct the policy of Governments and hold in the hollow of their hands the destiny of the people."

The United States initially resisted Central Banking

Unlike the European nations, the United States resisted central banking until the beginning of the twentieth century. Although several attempts were made by British Masonic bankers throughout the nineteenth century to institute central banking in the United States, there was no permanent central bank until 1913, when Congress passed the Federal Reserve Act. The first attempt to establish a central bank occurred in 1791. That year Congress granted a twenty-year charter to the Bank of the United States and sold shares to the public. The United States government bought twenty percent of the shares and Meyer Rothschild bought up most of the remaining stock. In 1811, when the charter came up for renewal, it was opposed by the state banks, and the Bank of the United States went out of business. Harvard history professor Charles Eliott Norton (1827–1908) observed that the War of 1812 was the way the Masonic oligarchy of England took vengeance on America for withdrawing from its international banking system. It is alleged by Norton that the war ended only when our government assured London that a central bank would be reestablished. At the head of the Bank of England during these negotiations was Nathan Rothschild.

In 1816, Congress granted another twenty-year charter to the second Bank of the United States.

Andrew Jackson, one of the heroes of the War of 1812, became president of the United States in 1829, voicing throughout his campaign his hatred for the central bank. Although a Mason himself, Jackson hated British control of the American money supply. He overlooked the fact that British banking and English Freemasonry were one. In 1833, Jackson ordered the secretary of the treasury to remove government deposits from the central bank and place them in state banks. On January 8, 1835, Jackson paid off the final installment of the national debt, the only president ever to do so. In 1836, when Congress renewed the bank's charter, Jackson vetoed it, openly accusing the bank of meddling in politics by granting loans to congressmen in an attempt to influence legislation. Jackson said that this amounted to a "bold effort" to control the government. His veto was sustained. With this popular move, Jackson won re-election.

The next president of the United States, William Henry Harrison, ran on the anti-Mason ticket.

On March 4, 1841, Harrison assumed office and a month later he mysteriously died. Vice President John Tyler, the son of a Mason, but not himself a Mason, immediately took over the presidency, the first to succeed to the office in this manner. Harrison's death was first attributed to acute intestinal distress, and then, variously, to "bilious pleurisy" and "pneumonia." History simply informs us that Harrison died of pneumonia. Ironically, Frederick May, a

Mason educated at Harvard by a Mason, was one of the two attending physicians, and he made sure no autopsy was performed on the robust hero of the War of 1812.

After Harrison's death, a greedy Congress, which had for three elections suffered from tack or campaign funds from the bankers, passed a bill restoring the Bank of the United States. President Tyler, however, following the wishes of Harrison, vetoed the bill and his veto was sustained.

London was livid, but could ill afford another war with America since she was in the throes of her First Opium War with China.

A Plan to Divide America

Upon the untimely death of Nathan Rothschild at age 59 in 1836, the scepter of power did not pass to Nathan's 28-year-old eldest son Lionel, who was ill-prepared, but rather to Nathan's brother James, head of the central band of Paris. When the U.S. Congress sustained President Tyler's veto for a central bank, Freemason Henry Palmerston turned to Paris for assistance.

Palmerston, who as the British Foreign Secretary working hard for the English Masonic drug lobby, expressed his interest to James Rothschild in a joint venture with French Freemasonry to capture America by intrigue. James immediately presented the proposal to the French Supreme Council of Freemasonry, reminding its monied members how easily they had increased their wealth during the Napoleonic Wars. While High Masons from all parts of Europe and Great Britain were attending six Masonic festivals held in Paris from 1841 to 1845, French Freemasonry also hosted for them six secret Supreme Council meetings, at which they would formulate a plan to divide America for conquest. Twenty years later their plan was manifested in the American Civil War.

Freemasonry and the American Civil War

To implement their plan to bring America under their control, English Freemasonry needed American Masons who were willing to betray their nation in exchange for political and/or esoteric power. Caleb Cushing and Albert Pike were chosen. Pike solicited assistance from a number of other Masons, including his Italian counterpart, Giuseppe Mazzini. Mazzini, as head of Italian Grand Orient Freemasonry, provide d revolutionary spirit. Pike, as Sovereign Grand Commander of the Southern Jurisdiction of Scottish Rite Freemasonry in America, organized the southern rebellion. And Cushing, a member of the Northern Jurisdiction of Freemasonry in America, financed the Southern insurrectionists through London's Masonic bankers.

In 1851, Giuseppe Mazzini began the process of provoking a civil war in America by establishing revolutionary groups across the country to intensify the debate on slavery. That year he sent his right-hand man Adriano Lemmi (1822–1896), and the great Masonic Magyar from Hungary, Louis Kossuth (1802–1894), to the United States to organize "Young America" lodges. The headquarters of their operation was Cincinnati Lodge n° 133. Lemmi returned to London that same year, while Kossuth stayed on. As subsequent events reveal, Kossuth completed a tour of several Masonic lodges to educate the Masonic hierarchy on how to recruit, organize, and train the youth in revolutionary strategy. According to Masonic documents, on February 28, 1852, Kossuth attended and addressed a meeting of Center Lodge n° 23, Indianapolis, and then traveled to St. John's Lodge n° 1 in Newark, N.J. On May 10, 1852 he addressed the Grand Lodge of Massachusetts.

Meanwhile, the Democratic nominating convention of 1852 was deadlocked among the leading presidential contenders because of the controversy over slavery. Franklin Pierce was selected as a compromise candidate because he opposed the divisive effects of anti-slavery agitation.

Kossuth, not an American citizen, shortly made contact with Pierce, offering him the propaganda services of Young America to promote his unity theme in his bid for the presidency if he would promise to appoint certain individuals to important posts. Pierce, not a Mason, was obviously ignorant of the fact that Young America was a nationwide group of abolitionist youth under the direction of Freemasonry—youth who were indoctrinated to promote division over slavery after the election. He was equally unaware that Kossuth's list of names were Masons and/or Masonic operatives organized to assure a split between the North and South, should Pierce appoint them. In his desire to become president, Pierce naively accepted Kossuth's offer.

Mazzini confirmed in his diary that Franklin Pierce was willing to accept help from Kossuth and his network of Masonic operatives:

> Kossuth and I are working with the very numerous Germanic element (Young America) in the United States for his (Pierce's) election, and under certain conditions which he has accepted. Of these conditions he has already fulfilled enough to give us security that he will carry out the rest.

The election of Pierce in 1853 as the fourteenth president of the United States was the signal for the new revolution in America to begin. As a coalition president, Pierce appointed both Southern planters and Northern businessmen to his cabinet. Mazzini wrote, "almost all his nominations are such as we desired."

Masons North and South

President Pierce's first appointment was Freemason Caleb Cushing (1800–1879) to the post of U.S. Attorney General. Not only was Cushing connected to English Freemasonry by his affiliation with the Northern Jurisdiction of Freemasonry, he was connected to the British opium trade through his father, a wealthy shipowner, and through his cousin, John Perkins Cushing, both of whom were engaged in the illicit opium traffic in China.

Caleb Cushing, a member of St. John's Lodge in Newburyport, Massachusetts, was a prolific writer against slavery. As U.S. attorney general, he became the master-architect of the Civil War.

His first Masonic assignment was to transfer money from British Masonic banker George Peabody to the Young America abolitionists, who after the elections were calling for the dissolution of the Union. Peabody, who owned a giant banking firm in England, hired the services of J.P. Morgan. Sr. (1837–1913) to handle the funds when they arrived in the United States. Upon Peabody's death, Morgan took over the firm and later moved it from England to the United States, renaming it Northern Securities. In 1869, Morgan went to London and reached an agreement to act as an agent for the N.M. Rothschild Company in the United States. When Morgan died in 1913, his son of the same name took over the firm.

The handler of the Peabody funds in London was Pierce's appointee to the U.S. Consulate, George Sanders. Sanders, not a Mason, but an enthusiast of Masonic revolutions, opened his London home to every debased revolutionary in Europe. In one gathering alone on February 21, 1854, Sanders hosted the following famous Masons: Giuseppe Mazzini; General Giuseppe Garibaldi; Louis Kossuth; Arnold Ruge, who with Karl Marx was the editor of a revolutionary magazine for Young Germany; Felice Orsine, one of Mazzini's contract terrorists and assassins; and Alexander Herzen of Russia, the man who initiated Freemason Mikhail Bakunin into Mazzini's Young Russia. Also present at that meeting was President Pierce's U.S. Ambassador to England, Freemason James Buchanan, destined to be the next president of the United States.

Since no evidence exists regarding the nature of this meeting, we can only speculate about it based upon subsequent events. It was likely concerned with the impending American Civil War.

For instance, five of the eight men present were directly involved in creating the southern insurrection. Sanders himself operated a cross-border spy ring for the Confederacy during the Civil War.

After the war, Sanders and his Canadian spies were indicted for allegedly helping to plan the assassination of Abraham Lincoln. Although charges were later dropped, Sanders's wanderings as a fugitive made him appear suspect. With men like Sanders, Peabody, and Morgan, Caleb Cushing was able to finance Young America abolitionists to instigate a civil war.

Sanders simply transferred Peabody's funds to Morgan and Morgan handed them over to Cushing.

At the same time, Cushing prepared for the British control of the Southern Jurisdiction of Scottish Rite Freemasonry, which had received its constitution from French Freemasonry. The man he selected for the task was Albert Pike. Pike had been Cushing's Masonic protégé in the 1820s when Pike was a school principal in Cushing's hometown of Newburyport, Massachusetts.

On March 20, 1853, two weeks after Cushing was appointed attorney general, he sent word to Pike (who was then living in Little Rock, Arkansas), to go to Charleston, South Carolina, and there receive the higher Masonic degrees (4th-32nd) from Albert Gallatin Mackey. Further instructions would be given him by Mackey. In 1857, Pike received the 33rd degree in New Orleans, and in 1859 he was elected Sovereign Grand Commander of the Supreme Council of the Southern Jurisdiction of Scottish Rite Freemasonry. The Northern Jurisdiction, which had been chartered under English Masonic obedience, now had one of its own controlling its rival.

At the head of the Northern Jurisdiction of Freemasonry was British spy and 33rd degree Freemason J.J.J. Gourgas (1777–1865). Gourgas had founded this "unauthorized" jurisdiction at the turn of the nineteenth century as a center for British espionage. In the early summer of 1813, when Gourgas's network was accidently discovered by the Southern Jurisdiction, he told his southern brothers:

> "Grand Lodges in the United States, if wise, ought to follow in the footsteps of the Grand Symbolic Lodge of England and

beware that with all their foreign intercourse and corresponding [meaning with French Freemasonry] that they do not become sooner or later Frenchified."

Although the southern Jurisdiction understood that the Northern Jurisdiction was under British Masonic obedience, Gourgas was permitted to operate north and east of the Ohio and Mississippi Rivers. Today this Masonic jurisdiction is referred to as the "Eastern Establishment."

In 1854, Gourgas assisted Freemason Killian Van Rensselaer in founding the Masonic front organization, the Knights of the Golden Circle in Cincinnati, Ohio. The Golden Circle immediately absorbed the Masonic operatives in Young America and became the military pre-organization of the Confederacy. The Knights of the Golden Circle rode west across Ohio, Indiana, and Illinois, then south along the Mississippi River to the Gulf of Mexico, and east into Maryland and Virginia.

Along the way they opened castles (chapters) and signed up recruits. Freemason John Gutman opened a castle of the Knights in Jackson, Mississippi. Likewise, Albert Pike opened one in New Orleans, through which Mazzini's Mafia would later enter the United States following the Civil War.

One of the recruits initiated into the Knights of the Golden Circle was General and Freemason P.T. Beauregard (1818–1893), a West Point graduate of 1838, and brother-in-law of Louisiana's political boss, Freemason John Slidell. Beauregard is credited with starting the Civil War with his surprise attack on Fort Sumter in 1861.

Long before Fort Sumter, however, Caleb Cushing realized that the anti-slavery north and the pro-slavery south were too far removed geographically to start a civil war over slavery. A division between neighbors in close proximity had to be created before a war would break out nationally.

Such a division was guaranteed by the first order of congressional business during the Pierce Administration—the passage of the Kansas-Nebraska Act. This act called for the Nebraska Territory to be divided into the territories of Kansas and Nebraska, whose residents would then determine whether slavery would be permitted or not. When the bill passed, the terrible aftermath was predictable. Outrageous acts of murder and arson were committed mostly by the pro-slavery Missourians, and savage cold-blooded massacres were committed by white abolitionists under the command of John Brown.

What is little known about John Brown (1800–1859) is that he spent much of his adult life in secret societies, including the Oddfellows, Sons of Temperance, and the Freemasons. Brown was made a Master Mason in Hudson Lodge No. 68, Hudson, Ohio, on May 11, 1824, and he served as junior deacon from 1825 to 1826. He renounced Freemasonry in 1830, when anti-Masonic fervor swept the nation. Caleb Cushing, however, viewed John Brown as the perfect candidate to bring about the insurrection of the Southern states. As an anti-Mason, Brown would never be suspected as being an agent of Freemasonry. John Brown had joined Young America during the Pierce Administration, and was supported financially by the John Jacob Astor Masonic interest in Boston and New York. After receiving instructions from Caleb Cushing, John Brown deliberately set out to instigate civil war in America.

In January 1857, Freemason James Buchanan was elected president to replace Franklin Pierce.

John A. Guitman, father of Mississippi Freemasonry and leader of the southern secessionists, was the representative from Mississippi in the House of Representatives. Guitman was slated to be the next Sovereign Grand Commander of the southern Jurisdiction of Scottish Rite Freemasonry, but on July 17, 1858, he suddenly died by poisoning, according to Masonic authority. Guitman's intimate friend Albert Pike, the man groomed by Cushing to take over Southern Freemasonry, conducted a lodge of sorrows in Guitman's memory, and a year later was elected to fill the post that Guitman would have held. Albert Pike then became the leader of the Southern secessionists.

Masonry and the Southern Confederacy

After Buchanan was elected president, he appointed to government posts those who were sure to start the Southern revolt. To the post of attorney general, Buchanan appointed Freemason Edwin M. Stanton of Pennsylvania, who would later be implicated in the assassination of President Abraham Lincoln. Buchanan appointed Freemason Howell Cobb of Georgia as secretary of the treasury. In March 1860, Cobb was elevated to the 33rd degree, and appointed by Albert Pike, leader of the secessionists in Georgia and chairman of the convention which organized the Confederacy in Montgomery, Alabama.

To the post of secretary of war, Buchanan appointed Freemason John B. Floyd, of St. Johns Lodge n° 36 in Richmond, Virginia. Two weeks before the 1860 presidential elections, Floyd quietly concluded an agreement with South Carolina's governor William Gist to sell 10,000 U.S. government rifles to his home state of South Carolina. In January 1861, Floyd was indicted in Washington, D.C., for giving aid while he was secretary of war to secessionist leaders. He demanded an immediate trial and that same month a committee of Masons from the House of Representatives exonerated him. That same year he was made brigadier general in the Confederate Army.

Buchanan's vice president was Freemason John C. Breckinridge Of Kentucky. Breckinridge was in attendance at the 1860 national convention of the Democratic party held at Charleston, S.C., the headquarters of the Southern Jurisdiction of Freemasonry. Presiding over the convention was Northern Jurisdiction Freemason Caleb Cushing. Under Cushing's supervision, the Gulf states delegation staged a walkout, formed their own convention, and elected Cushing as its chairman. The secessionists nominated Breckinridge as their candida te for president. On March 28, 1860, while campaigning in Kentucky, Breckinridge received the 33rd degree from Albert Pike.

Meanwhile, the newly formed Republican party nominated Abraham Lincoln as its presidential candidate. Lincoln, not a Mason, won the election. That same year Breckinridge was elected U.S. Senator from Kentucky. At the beginning of the Civil War, Breckinridge defended the South in the Senate and soon entered the Confederate service, for which act he was expelled from the Senate on December 4, 1861. Freemason Jefferson Davis, president of the Confederate States, appointed Breckinridge as his secretary of war.

It seems likely that Albert Pike had instigated the process of secession immediately after Lincoln's election. For example, on December 20, 1860, the state of South Carolina, headquarters of the Southern Jurisdiction of Freemasonry, was the first state to secede. On that same day, the state of Mississippi, whose secessionist organization had been created by the late Scottish Rite leader, John A. Guitman, followed South Carolina's lead. And on that same day, Freemason John Floyd, secretary of war under the still-presiding President Buchanan, performed another act of treason by ordering "the Allegheny arsenal at Pittsburgh to send 113 heavy columbian cannons and eleven 32-pound cannons to the unfinished, undefended U.S. forts at Ship Island, Mississippi, and Galveston, Texas, where they could be seized by the insurrectionists."

On December 22, 1860, the state of Florida followed suit and seceded from the Union, led by U.S. Senator David Levy Yulee, member of Hayward Lodge No. 7, Gainesville, Florida. The state of Alabama seceded on December 24, 1860. On January 2, 1861, Georgia's secession was led by two Freemasons, Howell Cobb, President Buchanan's secretary of the treasury, and Robert Toombs, who became the first secretary of state of the Confederacy. Both men received the honorary 33rd degree after the Civil War. Louisiana's secession occurred on January 7, 1861, led by two Freemasons, John Slidell and Pierre Soule. Soule also received the honorary 33rd degree after the Civil War. Backed by thousands of armed paramilitary Knights of the Golden Circle, forced Governor and Freemason Sam Houston to secede in February, 1861.

On April 12, 1861, General and Freemason P.T. Beauregard (1818–1893), a member of the Knights of the Golden Circle, was ordered to attack Fort Sumter, South Carolina. The American Civil War had begun. Anton Chaitkin writes:

> After Lincoln unexpectedly ordered a national mobilization to crush the rebellion, the Knights of the Golden Circle engaged in paramilitary and espionage operations in the North, along with parallel and successor groups under different names— none, however, publicly carried its proper name: Ancient and Accepted Scottish Rite of Freemasonry.

President Lincoln's inauguration was held on March 4, 1861. Of the appointments to his cabinet, he made one fatal judgment. He appointed Freemason Edwin Stanton, Buchanan's former attorney general, as his secretary of war. When Lincoln came to Washington to assume the presidency, Freemasonry's armed Knights of the Golden Circle were foiled by General Winfield Scott in their first of two attempts to assassinate Lincoln. Stanton would be implicated in the second and fatal attempt.

Masonic Banks and the North

Now that civil war was a reality, the same British Masonic financial interests who funded the South's insurrection, offered Lincoln the same assistance if he would authorize them to establish a central bank. Lincoln refused, realizing that to accept their funds would be to accept interest-bearing fiat money. The United States could print its own fiat money, interest free and debt free, and in February 1862, Lincoln issued the "Greenback."

Anticipating that President Lincoln would refuse to establish a central bank, England and France positioned their militaries to increase the pressure on Lincoln's government to accept a central bank on behalf of the combined European and British Masonic bankers. On November 8, 1861, England dispatched 8,000 troops to Canada, while France landed troops on the coast of Mexico.

The French imposed their choice of rulers on Mexico— Maximilian, brother of Emperor Joseph I Of Austria. Maximillian, who liked his Freemasonry more so than his Catholicity, accepted his assignment to permit the French to operate in Mexico against the United States.

President Lincoln was aware that this maneuver of the French and English was backed by the European and British bankers in their attempt to force a central bank on America. Not to be outflanked, Lincoln called on Czar Alexander II of Russia for assistance. Russia had a large navy, and the Czar had pledged his support to Lincoln prior to the beginning of the war. The Czar immediately issued orders to his imperial navy to sail for the American ports or New York City and San Francisco, telling his admirals to take their orders from Lincoln. The ships began arriving in September, 1863. After the Civil War, Russia sent a bill to the United States in the amount of $7.2 million, but Congress had never authorized the hiring of the Russian Fleet. Lincoln's Secretary of State William H. Seward, a vocal anti-Mason who had run for state senate as an anti Masonic candidate, solved this legal problem by negotiating the purchase of a worthless piece of real estate for the amount of the bill submitted by Russia. This became known as "Seward's Folly," and in 1867 Alaska became the newest territory of the United States.

Lincoln had played a deadly game, and with Russian troops on American shores, he won. England and France, not wishing to go to war with Russia over our Civil War, withdrew their troops from Canada and Mexico. The Masonic bankers did not give up. In July 1862, an agent of the London bankers sent a letter to the leading financiers and bankers of America informing them that the greenback would put the American Masonic bankers out of business if they did not act fast.

London wanted American bankers to pressure Congress to issue bonds that would be "used as a banking basis." The message said in part: "It will not do to allow the greenback(s), as [they are] called, to circulate as money any length of time, for we cannot control them. But we can control the bonds and through them the bank issues." The instructions were urgent. The American financiers were not to wait on treasury Secretary Salmon P. Chase to make his recommendations to Congress. They were instead to meet with the congressmen and senators in lodge, where they could discuss the matter in private.

Even President Lincoln, as resolute as he was in frustrating every move of the Masonic bankers of Europe to establish a central bank in America, could not hold at bay a greedy Congress. On February 25, 1863, Congress passed the National Banking Act, which created a federally chartered national bank that had the power to issue U.S. Bank Notes. These notes were, in fact, money created by private bankers to be loaned to the government at interest paper money supported not by gold but by debt. This bill was supported and urged by the Secretary of the Treasury, Salmon P. Chase. Years later, British Freemasonry posthumously honored Salmon P. Chase by naming a bank after him, the Chase Bank, which became the Chase Manhattan Bank, owned by David Rockefeller.

After passage of the National Banking Act, Lincoln once again warned the American people against the central bank, the "money power" as he called it, with these sobering words: The money power preys upon the nation in times of peace and conspires against it in times of adversity. It is more despotic than monarchy, more insolent than autocracy, more selfish than bureaucracy. I see in the near future a crisis approaching that unnerves me, and causes me to tremble for the safety of my country. Corporations have been enthroned, an era of corruption will follow, and the money power of the country will endeavor to prolong its reign by working upon the prejudices of the people, until the wealth is aggregated in a few hands, and the republic is destroyed.

A few months after the passage of the bill, the Rothschild bank in England wrote a letter to the New York bankers which expressed the contempt in which the Masonic elite held the people and their interests:

The few who understand the system [interest-bearing fiat money] will either be so interested in its profits, or so dependent on its favors that there will be no opposition from that class, while on the other hand, the great body of people, mentally incapable of comprehending the tremendous advantages that capital derives from the system, will bear its burdens without complaint, and perhaps without even suspecting the system is inimical to their interests.

A Hatred of America

Apart from the profits to be made from banking during the war, fortunes were made in many other ways. One way to accumulate wealth was to run the Union blockade against the Confederacy. British Freemason Thomas W. House, whose parents were Jewish, and whose father was an agent for the Rothschild bank in England, made his fortune smuggling arms by ship from Britain, through the Union blockade, to Texas. After the war, House returned to England and gave his son, Edward Mandell House (1858–1938), an anti-American, pro-Marxist education at Bath. While in England, Edward House joined English Freemasonry Years later Edward House returned to Texas to tend his father's cotton plantations. There he received the 33rd degree. Although born in America, and returning later in life to reap the benefits of America's fertile land, "Colonel" House (a title he gave himself) despised the United States as an enemy land, and retained a fierce loyalty to Great Britain. He planned one day to destroy single-handedly, not only the United States of America, but Russia as well, for he despised imperial Russia as much as he did America for its part in assisting Lincoln during the Civil War. A 1912 novel that House wrote, entitled *Philip Dru: Administrator: A Story of Tomorrow*, expresses the loathing House felt for his country of birth:

> America is the most undemocratic of democratic countries...
> Our Constitution and our laws served us well for the first

hundred years of our existence, but under the conditions of to-day they are not only obsolete, but even grotesque.

Chapter 5

GRADUALISM: GOLD, DOLLARS, DEBT, and DRUGS

The drug and arms traffic is run by the mafia at the operational level and by British Freemasonry at the financial level...

Marco Fanini—Milan, Italy

The Masonic Assassination of Abe Lincoln

There are two reasons why the British Masonic conspiracy plunged America into civil war. First, British bankers wanted to establish a permanent central bank under their total control. Second, British Freemasonry wanted to divide powerful America into two weak nations for easy conquest. Information on the latter half of the plan was first published in The Present Attempt to Dissolve the American Union: A British Aristocratic Plot (1862), by Samuel Morse (1791–1872), an American artist and inventor, who was also an American counterintelligence specialist. Had it not been for Abraham Lincoln, English Freemasonry would have succeeded. When Lincoln restored the Union, the British Brotherhood, out of revenge, plotted his assassination. The Knights of the Golden Circle, bankrolled by British Masonic interests, selected John Wilkes Booth, a 33rd degree Mason and member of Mazzini's Young America, for the task. Freemason Edwin Stanton was assigned to cover up Masonic involvement in the crime.

Immediately after Lincoln's assassination, Stanton ordered military blockades on all roads out of Washington, D.C., except one the road Booth was known to have taken for his escape route.

Stanton then arranged for a drunk man to be found, similar in build and appearance to Booth.

This man was to be murdered and his body burned in a barn adjacent to the only road not guarded by the military. Stanton just happened to be on that road when he "found" the murdered man, certifying that the charred body was the remains of John Wilkes Booth. The real John Wilkes Booth escaped.

After these events, the Knights were soon exposed to the Military Commission that heard evidence on the Lincoln assassination as the secret force behind both the Civil War and the assassination. Original documents relating to the president's assassination are still locked up in the archives of the Defense Department and are not available to researchers today. However, significant information which implicates the Knights comes from on-the-scene reporters at the June 2–28, 1865, Indianapolis conspiracy trial. Directly involved in the plot were the following individuals: 33rd degree Freemason and British Prime Minister Henry Palmerston (died in 1865); 33rd degree Freemason John Wilkes Booth; Freemason Judah P. Benjamin, the British Masonic banker's mouthpiece who gave the order for Lincoln's assassination; and Jacob Thompson, former Interior Secretary in the Buchanan administration, who withdrew $180,000 from the Bank of Montreal in Canada to set the plot in motion. (Benjamin and Thompson both fled to England to avoid apprehension.) And Freemason Edwin Stanton prepared a cover-up that compares in audacity with the 1963 Warren Commission cover-up of the Kennedy assassination.

The exposure of the Knights was so celebrated following the 1865 conspiracy trials that in the spring of 1867, Albert Pike and a small group of former Confederate generals met in the Maxwell House Hotel in Nashville, Tennessee, to change the name of the Knights of the Golden Circle to the Knights of the Ku Klux Klan.

Two books from the turn of the twentieth century document Pike's direct involvement in founding the Klan: Ku Klux Klan: Its Origin, Growth and Disbandment (1905) by J.C. Lester and D.L. Wilson; and Authentic History: Ku Klux Klan 1865–1877 (1924) by Susan Lawrence Davis. According to these sources, the Knight's new name was taken from the Greek word kuklos, which means "circle." On April 16, 1868, Albert Pike wrote an editorial in the Memphis Daily Appeal, calling for a white "Order of Southern Brotherhood," which amounted to nothing more than a subtle advertisement for the Klan.

Under its new name, the Klan attempted to rekindle the Civil War by instigating riots throughout the South. Freemason Andrew Johnson, who assumed the presidency following Lincoln's assassination, understood these riots were an attempt to incite another Civil War. As a Master Mason Johnson, however, was not privy to the activity of the 33rd degree Supreme Council and could not see the hand of Freemasonry in the riots. He was as equally ignorant of the fact that the notorious outlaw Jesse James (1847–1882) was a 33rd degree Freemason and a member of the Knights of the Golden Circle, which had been assigned the task by Albert Pike of robbing Northern banks to fund this new war.

Of course, the attempt to incite another civil war was unsuccessful. But what of the gold stolen by the James gang? Ralph Epperson, who confirmed in *The Unseen Hand* that both James and Booth were high degree Masons, writes: "It has been estimated that Jesse and the other members of the Knights had buried over $7 billion in gold all over the western states." This gold has never been found.

A New British Strategy: Gradualism

Although the National Banking Act of 1863 gave the British bankers a foothold in American finance, it did not accomplish their full intent—total control of the money supply. Three problems, according to British bankers, were inherent in the National Banking Act of 1863: (1) As long as America held gold reserves Congress would hold power over the money supply; (2) State banks, which were not controlled by the National Bank, were still permitted to issue their own currency; and (3) the National Bank had inadequate reserves.

British bankers wanted to establish a central bank under their total control—a bank that would not be controlled by Congress; a bank that would have jurisdiction over state banks; and a bank that would either hold in its vaults the gold reserves of the United States of America, or operate without a gold-convertible currency, permitting bankers to print an unlimited amount of fiat money and loan it at interest. The failure of the Civil War to divide America coupled with the National Banking Act's protection of Americans' assets, temporarily derailed British bankers in their plan to get a firm and permanent hold on the money supply in America. Their plot, however, continued.

Meanwhile, the American economy began to flourish, as it has after every war. In 1876 America entered its period of industrial boom with the invention of the telephone, the automobile in the 1890s, and the airplane in 1903. Railroads, forged by new steel mills, crisscrossed the nation.

This was the heyday of the American free enterprise system. The famous phrase, "the American dream," was coined during these years.

On the other side of the ocean, the bankers of British Masonry developed a new strategy for capturing American banking: "gradualism." They could do little else, given that the house of Rothschild was preoccupied with more important financial ventures in South Africa—diamonds and gold—the only currency acceptable to opium farmers in the Orient. English Freemasonry's plan for America would wait.

But these were the days of a new breed of English Freemason, spearheaded by John Ruskin, followed by Cecil Rhodes and Alfre Milner. These men, and those who surrounded them, realized why English Freemasonry had failed in its attempt to take over the finances of America. Money power alone was not enough. A political base had to be gradually and secretly constructed in America that would be controlled by London. That secret political base began with the British Round Table and its offshoot think-tanks discussed fully in Chapter three. By cultivating, supporting, and advancing the careers of this new breed of English Mason. British Masons successfully laid the political groundwork with their front organizations to influence Americas politicians. This new breed would later vote on establishing a privately owned central bank in the United States that would give the British bankers all they would ask for.

The Federal Reserve Bank

The Masons initiated their new plan immediately after our Civil War. In 1869, when Cecil Rhodes (age sixteen) first took ship to South Africa to mine for gold and diamonds, British banker Lionel Rothschild (1808–1879) contracted with J.P. Morgan to form the American-based Northern Securities Company to act as an agent for N.M. Rothschild and Sons in the United States.

The house of Rothschild was also working with the house of Warburg of Frankfurt, Germany, where the three Warburg brothers (Max, Felix and Paul), were funding Grand Orient Freemasonry's revolutions on the Continent. Felix Warburg's father-in-law was Jacob Schiff, also a Grand Orient Mason. While J.P. Morgan was in London negotiating an agency position in America for the house of Rothschild, Max Warburg, in conjunction with the house of Rothschild, sent Jacob Schiff to the United States to buy into the existing banking firm of Kuhn, Loeb & Co.

Through Kuhn-Loeb, the house of Rothschild and the house of Warburg financed the business endeavors of the following men: John D. Rockefeller in creating the Standard Oil empire, Freemason Edward Harriman in building railroads, and Andrew Carnegie in constructing steel mills. Paul Warburg and his brother Felix immigrated to the United States in 1902. Both became partners in Kuhn, Loeb and Company, with Paul drawing an annual salary of $500,000. Paul Warburg was the Mason most responsible for creating the Federal Reserve Bank, America's permanent central bank established by Congress in 1913.

In order to impress upon the minds of certain bankers in the hinterland of America the need for a federal banking system, the British-controlled New York bankers (euphemistically known as "Wall Street") created a series of financial crises beginning in 1893 and continuing through the banking panic of 1907. The man in charge of starting these panics was J.P. Morgan, who did so simply by spreading rumors about the instability of certain banks. These strategic rumors would end in mini-runs on the banks that Wall Street was trying to whip into submission to back its plan for a privately owned central banking system—a banking system that would control fiscal policy for all America. Thirty-second degree Freemason and Senator Robert Owen (1856–1947), a co-author of the Federal Reserve Act (who later deeply regretted his role), testified before a congressional committee on how Morgan engineered the panics. While president of the First National Bank of Muskogee, Ok., Owen said he received from the National Bankers' Association headquartered in New York what came to be known as the "Panic Circular of 1893." It stated:

> "You will at once retire one-third of your circulation and call in one-half of your loans".

There was no need for tightening credit or recalling loans. It was simply a technique used by British Masonic bankers on Wall Street to create panic. A story in *Life magazine* in April 25, 1949, by historian Frederick Lewis Allen, confirms Morgan's role in spreading these rumors about the insolvency of the Knickerbocker Bank and The Trust Company of America, which rumors triggered the 1907 panic. Moreover, Freemason and Congressman Louis T. McFadden (1876–1936), president of the First National Bank of Canton, PA., as well as head of the House Banking and Currency Committee for ten years, confirmed that Morgan took his orders from the British Rothschilds.

The "panic" Morgan had created, he also ended single-handedly. He had made his point.

Frederick Allen explains:

> "The lesson of the Panic of 1907 was clear, though not for some six years was it destined to be embodied in legislation: the United States gravely needed a central banking system..."

While J.P. Morgan was creating bank panics, Paul Warburg was writing and lecturing across America on the need for "banking reforms" to prevent such crises. His reforms called for a central bank to control credit. Working with Warburg was Freemason Nelson Aldrich (1841–1915), a senator from Providence, Rhode Island. (John D. Rockefeller, Sr. [1839–1937] married the daughter of Senator Aldrich). After the banking panic of 1907, Senator Aldrich was appointed by the Senate to head the National Monetary Commission to tour Europe on a fact-finding mission about central banking. The commission consisted of the following Wall Street financial power brokers: Paul Warburg, partner in Kuhn, Loeb & Co.; Frank Vanderlip, president of Kuhn-Loeb's National Bank of New York; Henry Davidson, senior partner of J.P. Morgan; Charles Norton, president of Morgan's First National Bank of New York; and Benjamin Strong, president of Morgan's Banker's Trust Company.

After two years touring Europe, the commission returned to America in 1909. In 1910 Senator Aldrich called a secret meeting to be held at a resort on Jekyll Island, Georgia, owned by J.P. Morgan. Attending the meeting were A. Piatt Andrew, assistant secretary of the treasury, all the fact-finding members of the commission, including Nelson Aldrich and Paul Warburg, and a representative from Rockefeller's National City Bank. This coterie of Masonic bankers wrote the final recommendations for the commission's report, which included the creation of a federal banking system and the permanent suspension of gold-convertible money. Warburg stressed in the report and in discussion of its recommendations, that the term "central bank" should not be used. Instead, the federal bank had to be seen as a "regional reserve" with branches in different sections of the country. It would be called the Federal Reserve System so that the populace would believe that it was held by the federal government.

One obstacle lay ahead. A Republican president was in the White House. The public believed that Republicans were connected with the money brokers of Wall Street, and they would suspect the Federal Reserve Act if a Republican president were pushing for its passage. On the other hand, a Democrat in the White House supporting the passage of the Federal Reserve Act would be viewed as "stripping Wall Street of its power." Since elections were only two years away, the commission delayed presenting their report to Congress.

Meanwhile, in 1909, the John D. Rockefeller Standard Oil empire had grown so large that the U.S. Supreme Court perceived a money power conspiracy of the magnitude foreseen by President Abraham Lincoln in 1863.

The Supreme Court took a firm hand against the oil baron. To break up what it perceived as a conspiracy against the sovereignty of the nation, the Court's decree stated: "Rockefeller's Standard Oil Company must be dissolved at once. For the safety of the Republic we now decree that the dangerous conspiracy must be ended by November 15, 1911.

Although Rockefeller was forced to break up his huge oil monopoly into smaller companies, the Supreme Court had cut off only one tentacle of the octopus. Although the monopoly was divided into smaller panics with Rockefeller puppets controlling each little corporation, the larger conspiracy was not touched. More dangerous than the Rockefeller oil empire were the Wall Street conspirators at Jekyll Island—conspirators backed by British and European Masonic bankers. When these men returned from the island, one job remained they must find a man willing to bend to their influence in exchange for the prestige of being president of the United States of America. Woodrow Wilson was the perfect presidential candidate for the Wall Street Masonic bankers. Although not a Mason himself, he admired members of the Craft, and for twenty years before his nomination he moved in their shadow. Moreover, in 1907, while Morgan was spreading rumors of a banking crisis, Wilson was full of praise for Morgan's role in American society. Morgan suggested to Paul Warburg that Wilson might be their candidate for the presidency. Warburg approached Wilson with the idea, confirming to him that funds were no obstacle. Warburg then introduced "Colonel" Edward Mandell House to Wilson, stating that "Colonel" House would be Wilson's mouthpiece.

In 1912, Wilson's campaign speech was on cue. Constantly at his side was "Colonel" House.

While Wilson promised reform of the banking and currency system, he also denounced the concept of central banking. This the voters wanted to hear, and this "Colonel" House instructed Wilson to say. To assure the vote of Americans who believed all they heard, Woodrow Wilson campaigned against Wall Street with a vengeance. "I will lead the fight against those wolves of Wall Street," he proclaimed. Voters, mindful of the 1909 Supreme Court action against the powerful Wall Street oil baron, John D. Rockefeller, elected Democrat Wilson as the twenty-eighth President of the United States of America.

After his inauguration on March 4, 1913, Woodrow Wilson, however, set out to establish what he had promised he would fight against—a central bank. This time he informed the public that the establishment of a central bank would smash the power of Wall Street. Three months later, on June 23, 1913, the Federal Reserve Act was introduced to Congress and hotly debated for the next six months. Finally, on December 22, 1913, an exhausted Congress, desiring to go home for Christmas, voted for passage—298 to 60 in the House, and 43 to 25 in the Senate. The two Masons who helped pilot the Federal Reserve Act through Congress were 32nd degree Mason, Senator William G. McAdoo (1863–1941), appointed by Wilson to the position of Secretary of the Treasury from 1913 to 1918, and 33rd degree Mason, Senator Carter Glass (1858–1946), chairman of the House Banking and Currency

Committee (later to be Secretary of the Treasury in 1918 under Wilson). Finally, on December 22, 1913, an exhausted Congress, desiring to go home for Christmas, voted for passage—298 to 60 in the House, and 43 to 25 in the Senate.

The two Masons who helped pilot the Federal Reserve Act through Congress were 32nd degree Mason, Senator William G. McAdoo (18,631,941), appointed by Wilson to the position of Secretary of the Treasury from 1913 to 1918, and 33rd degree Mason, Senator Carter Glass (1858–1946), chairman of the House Banking and Currency Committee (later to be Secretary of the Treasury in 1918 under Wilson).

During this entire period, Paul Warburg and "Colonel" House maintained constant contact.

House, the Masonic mentor and mouthpiece for Wilson, is regarded by many historians as the real president of the United States during the Wilson years. "Colonel" House had never served in any military; his title was honorary. He never held an elected position in American politics before or after Wilson's election. He was an Englishman schooled in the communist philosophies of Marx and Engels. House once wrote of establishing "socialism as dreamed by Karl Marx." He was a 33rd degree English Freemason who so hated the United States of America that he vowed to topple it single-handedly with Marxist-style socialism. "Colonel" House was the man in whom the Schiffs, the Warburgs, the Kahns, the Rockefellers, and the Morgans had put their faith. He did not let them down. President Woodrow Wilson later wrote, "House's thoughts and mine are one."

Who Owns the Fed?

The *Encyclopaedia Britannica* describes the Federal Reserve banking system as consisting of twelve banks located in twelve Federal Reserve districts, each of which "is a privately owned corporation established pursuant to the Federal Reserve Act to serve the public interest; it is governed by a board of nine directors, six of whom are elected by the member banks and three of whom are appointed by the Board of Governors of the Federal Reserve System." Nowhere in this account, nor in any other description, is it recorded that the Federal Reserve System, or the Fed, is owned by our government. It is a popular misconception that our government controls the Fed. In fact, the Fed is kind enough to permit the President of the United States to appoint the Chairman of the Board of the Fed only when the previous chairman resigns or dies. This presidential appointee is selected from current board members, who have already been elected by member banks. Our government never has, nor does it now own, control, or influence the decisions made by the Federal Reserve Board. The Board's only duty is to make a profit for its private stockholders. It is, therefore, ludicrous to suggest, as does the British-owned *Encyclopaedia Britannica,* that the Fed "serves the public interest." To the contrary. The Fed has financially exploited both our government and our citizenry as we shall see.

Who Benefits from a Central Bank?

Central banks are credit banks only, with no function in savings, commerce, or investments. Their business it to loan money. Hence, it is to a central bank's advantage to keep a government spending and borrowing. It is what state socialism is all about— not for the benefit of the poor, as we are led to believe, but for the profit of corporate socialism. If a government refuses to go along with this program, the central bank simply plunges the nation into recession or depression by "manipulation of exchanges, gold flows, discount rates, and even levels of business activity."

This manipulation forces a government to borrow.

Once a government gives authority to a central banking system to control all national credit, member banks automatically become subordinate to the central bank. The central bank maintains this subordination by loaning money at prime (discount) interest rates.

The central bank also sets the prime rate. Member banks, in turn, loan to the public at higher interest rates.

The net worth of central banks, therefore, is calculated in terms of debt-backed dollars, not gold backed dollars. Gold backed dollars (or gold-convertible currency, as it is normally called), is hazardous to the future of central banking, and central banks and those who run them have always opposed a monetary system where currency can be converted to gold on demand. Such a system requires a certain percentage of gold permanently on deposit to meet the convertible demand. This gold cannot be invested or loaned, and thus it is useless to a credit bank. Retaining the gold standard is acceptable, however, as long as the central bank, and not the government, owns the reserves. A gold standard, as opposed to a gold-convertible currency, stabilizes the value of the base currency, while permitting the circulation of fiat money in excess of the bank's gold reserves.

Although President Woodrow Wilson fulfilled his pledge to the Masonic bankers by supporting the establishment of the Federal Reserve System, there were still many patriotic congressmen who distrusted Wall Street. These patriots insisted that our currency remain gold-convertible.

Hence, Congress did not completely adhere to the Jekyll Island program, and retained a gold convertible currency. This, in effect, kept the private bankers from printing an unlimited supply of fiat money. At the time Paul Warburg remarked to "Colonel" House, "Well, we haven't got quite everything we want, but the lack can be adjusted later by administrative process".

The Stock Market Crash of 1929

The Great Depression, which began with the stock market crash in 1929, was created by the Fed.

For over a century, British bankers had manipulated financial cycles to create alternate periods of inflation and deflation in order to increase their wealth. They were now poised to make a major killing by manipulating the American stock market for the purpose of forcing our government to abandon gold-convertible currency. Between 1923 and 1929, the Federal Reserve expanded the money supply by 62 percent. Many investors took advantage of this easy-money, borrowing and buying stocks, a process that pushed the stock market to dizzying heights.

A few concerned congressmen in 1928 scheduled hearings on stabilizing the dollar. At the hearings evidence was disclosed that in 1927, the Federal Reserve Board and heads of the European central banks had planned, at a secret luncheon, a major stock market crash. However, the majority of congressmen were Masons (69 percent of the House and 63 percent of the Senate), so no action was taken against the Fed. Calvin Coolidge was then president, and while not a Mason himself, he was so impressed with them that his entire cabinet were Masons.

Among them, serving as his secretary of the treasury, was Royal Arch Mason Andrew Mellon, president of Mellon National Bank of Pittsburgh, Pennsylvania. On February 6, 1929, British Freemason Montagu Norman, Governor of the Bank of England, came to Washington to confer with Andrew Mellon. Immediately after the meeting, the Federal Reserve Board reversed its easy-money policy and began to raise the discount rate. Based upon these and subsequent events, we can deduce that in this meeting with Mellon, British Freemasonry was deliberately directing a course that would bring financial disaster and terrible hardship upon an entire nation: for the purpose of forcing its government to relinquish its gold reserves. It was not only proper Masonic banking protocol to inform brother Andrew Mellon of the plot so he would know when to get out of the stock market, it also made political sense to keep Mellon financially solvent lest he shut down their scheme through countermeasures, such as closing the stock market until things cooled down.

On March 9, 1929, Freemason Paul Warburg signaled all member banks to get out of the stock market or sell short. If they acted immediately, they would reap enormous profits as the Dow Jones plunged' Mellon's bank was the first to follow Warburg's advice. Seven months later, on October 24, 1929, the money balloon—which had been inflated constantly by the Fed for nearly seven years—exploded. The new President, Republican Herbert Hoover, was not exploded, but his Treasury Secretary was the same Royal Arch Mason appointed by his predecessor—Andrew Mellon, the man who evidently was first informed of the timing of the stock market crash.

The mechanics of the stock market crash are as follows: New York's Masonic financiers called 24-hour broker call loans. Stock brokers and their customers were forced to dump their stock on the market in order to pay off the loans. Non-member banks were heavily involved in broker call claims. Runs soon exhausted coin and currency, forcing banks to close. The Federal Reserve refused to come to their aid, although under law it had been instructed to do so. For the next four and a half years our nation was plunged into deep depression. Meanwhile, member banks, informed in advance by the Masonic oligarchy to sell short, bought up all the deflated Wall Street stock. Overnight the wealth of the common citizen was transferred to the British banking conspirators for pennies on the dollar. Then they went after our gold.

Predictably, Republican President Herbert Hoover was blamed for the catastrophe. This fact all but guaranteed that the next president would be a Democrat—voted in by a citizenry that believed the lie that Democrats are for the poor and Republicans are for the rich.

British Masonic Bankers Confiscate U.S. Citizens' Gold

Although the depression was severe, the gold coins and gold-convertible currency still held by the American citizen made him independent, and thus still free from financial control by the Masonic Bankers of England. The next Democratic president of the United States would be an accomplice to the Fed's scheme and correct this situation, promising to solve the problem caused by the outgoing Republican administration. On March 1, 1933, 32nd degree Freemason Franklin D. Roosevelt became the thirty second president of the United States of America. His treasury secretary was 33rd degree Freemason Henry Morgenthau.

Franklin Roosevelt adopted two banking policies, called the Banking Act of 1933 and the Banking Act of 1935, that gave British Masonic bankers control of our gold supply. The first would take our currency off the gold-backed dollars; the second would permit the Fed to own the gold confiscated from the citizens. Both acts increased the revenue of the Fed by over $100 million.

On April 5, 1933, after one month in Office, Roosevelt issued an executive order requiring American citizens to surrender gold coins, gold bullion, and gold certificates—not to the nearest United States mint or depository, but to the nearest privately Owned Federal Reserve Bank. The Fed redeemed the gold for $20.67 an Ounce. After the citizens' gold was confiscated, the U.S. government increased the value of gold to $35.00 an ounce.

Who made the $14.33 profit per ounce? The privately owned Federal Reserve Bank, of course.

Here is how it worked. In late 1933, the Federal Reserve turned over the surrendered gold, for which it had paid $20.67 per ounce, to United States mints. In exchange, the Fed received Series 1934 gold certificates each with a nominal value of $100,000 issued on the increased value of $35 an ounce from the U.S. Treasury. On the obverse of the certificates was printed the following statement: "This is to certify that there is on deposit in the Treasury of the United States one hundred thousand dollars in gold payable to bearer on demand as authorized by law." The Fed had paid approximately $200 million for the citizen's gold. Six months later, when the gold was delivered to the United States mints, the Fed received Series 1934 gold certificates totaling in value over $300 million. A hefty profit of over $100 million dollars was realized in six months by the British banking fraternity simply for collecting, holding, and returning gold that was not theirs.

Roosevelt's publicly stated purpose for the confiscation of our gold and the elimination of gold-backed currency was to pull us out of depression. Gold-backed dollars cannot be inflated, for gold, a hard-medal commodity, is fixed in value, requiring it to be held in reserve for conversion on demand. The massive government spending necessary to break the back of the depression required fiat money, just as in time of war. The danger of printing an unlimited supply of paper currency, of course, was the creation of inflation in addition to long-term debt. In the short-term, however, the nation would be put back to work.

This plan to move the United States out of the Great Depression did not sound so bad. The truth was, however, that to eliminate our gold-convertible currency benefited only the Fed, since it alone was given permission to print fiat money. Only the Fed could loan fiat money to private banks and governments and charge interest. The real purpose of the two banking acts, therefore, was to make the Masonic banking fraternity wealthier. The Encyclopaedia Britannica admits that the centralization of control by the Federal Reserve Bank's Board of Governors was significantly increased by Roosevelt's two Banking Acts.

From then on, the ease with which our government could borrow and spend money became habit-forming. Deficit-spending, which had indebted our government by $1 billion following World War Il, increased our debt by the time we reached the moon in 1969 to $100 billion. By the end of the Carter administration our national debt had reached $500 billion. By the end of the Reagan-Bush administrations it was over $4 trillion, most of which was spent on military technology for the express purpose of bankrupting the Soviet Union (which could not compete and was forced to dismantle). The fall of the Soviet empire realized, the bankers began looking for other reasons to loan money to our spend-crazy government. Anglophile Clinton, a Rhodes Scholar trained on the "merits" of deficit spending by British Masonic professor, came to their rescue in his attempt to get the National Health Care Act passed. Republicans, however, saw through this insane act, and put it to rest—temporarily.

Who benefits from our deficit spending? Democrats say the poor benefit. But, as we have demonstrated, only wealthy English Freemasonry and its members' credit banks benefit. If our national debt is paid off, and our government lives within its means, the central banks will go broke—an unconscionable thought. It is therefore to the advantage of central bankers to encourage deficit spending, falsely promoting it as a means to create jobs and make people rich.

Just the opposite is true, however. Taxes have increased to pay for an ever-expanding debt. The heavier tax burden saps the wealth of our nation, placing in the hands of the Masonic banking monopoly of London, England, the destiny of our people. The peril that central banking presents to sovereign nations is summed up by Meyer Rothschild: "Permit me to control the money of a nation, and I care not who makes its laws".

The Gold Power of the United States of America

Although the U.S. dollar was no longer gold-convertible by 1935, the dollar was, and still is, the most powerful currency in the world because of our gold reserves. Always sagacious, prior to World War Il the Fed knew that the impending world war would bring more gold into the United States' Treasury, because payments between nations during war are made in good delivery gold (meaning .995 fineness). America would be the major supplier of materiel in the Allied war effort. As a result, by 1941 our nation owned almost two-thirds of the world's good delivery gold stock valued at $24 billion; our printed money supply was only $42 billion, a ratio of gold to paper better than 1:2; our national debt was $40 billion, as opposed to over $4 trillion today; our monthly short term obligations to foreigners were only $3 to $4 billion (a favorable balance of payments), as opposed to ten times that amount today.

Although the Fed and its controlling British Masonic bankers had control of our gold, it planned to wait until after the war to devise a plan to abscond legally with the entire stockpile. Hitler, meanwhile, would steal for them the gold reserves of the European nations, as we shall soon see.

A World Bank: The Bank for International Settlements

There is an underlying reason for the confiscation of the world's gold by English Freemasonry that has not been addressed by any other conspiracy researcher but this author alone. We must remember that the only mediums of exchange acceptable to the opium farmers in the Orient are gold or diamonds. The primary industry of Great Britain was and still is, the drug industry, which requires the movement of massive amounts gold bullion to the Orient. Second to English Freemasonry's drug industry is its banking industry. One industry cannot Survive without the other.

Meanwhile, as the British Masonic-controlled Federal Reserve Bank was confiscating the gold of American citizens in 1933, it had in 1930 already established a bank in Europe for the same purpose. The Bank for International Settlements (BIS) in Basel, Switzerland, was poised to receive the gold reserves of European nations during World War Il for safekeeping in Switzerland. Dr. Carroll Quigley, in his massive book, Tragedy and Hope, informs us that the BIS was "a private bank owned and controlled by the world's central banks which were themselves private corporations "45 The Encyclopaedia Britannica agrees with Quigley, but adds that the BIS was an "international bank established at Basel, Switzerland in 1930 as the agency to handle the payment of reparations by Germany after World War I" as specified by the Versailles Treaty in 1919.

We should note the eleven year gap between the Versailles Treaty and the founding of the BIS.

In June 1919, following World War I, the Versailles Treaty had mandated that Germany make war reparations. Surely it would be ludicrous to establish a collection agency for war reparations ten years after the agreement which set terms, and one year following the world's worse financial crash. In 1929, Germany had no funds with which to pay reparations. Furthermore, in 1931, one year after the BIS was founded, all the European powers, except France, had ended reparations demands. Two years later, Hitler repudiated all reparations.

Hitler and the BIS

If not to collect reparations, what actually was the function of the BIS? Recent information uncovered by British historian Charles Higham and published in his book *Trading with the Enemy* (1983), states that the BIS

> "was to be a money funnel for American and British funds to flow into Hitler's coffers and to help Hitler build up his war machine".

This is a shocking claim to make, but stockholders in the Bank for International Settlements did share something in common. The major stockholder in the BIS was the Bank of England whose major stockholder, in turn, was the house of Rothschild, which controlled finances for the Round Table groups. Other owners included the Morgan-affiliated First National Bank of New York, the Reichsbank of Germany, the Bank of Italy, the Bank of France, and other central banks. Many of the individuals who were associated with the BIS and named by Higham in his book were either known Masons and/or members of the Round Table groups (although he does not mention that fact). Moreover, Hjalmar Schacht, Hitler's Minister of Economics and president of the Reichsbank, was a closet English Freemason, who urged British bankers to establish the BIS to fund Hitler's war. In fact, part of the Bank's charter, and assented to by the respective governments involved in the BIS's establishment, was that the BIS should be immune from seizure, closure, or censure, whether or not its owners were at war.

What could possibly motivate British bankers to finance the arming of Hitler's Germany?

According to Higham, the BIS financed Hitler as a means to another end: to sweep and garner the gold of Europe for the benefit of what Higham calls "The Fraternity." The Fraternity, of course, is just another name for Freemasonry. And Freemasonry, as an international organization, has always seen itself as above and beyond the laws of any nation. Hitler was to loot the gold reserves of nations conquered by the Nazi Army and deposit the gold in the Bank for International Settlements (BIS) in Switzerland. The plunder began in March 1938, a year before World War Il began, when Hitler's troops marched into Austria. One of their first acts was to remove the gold from Austrian banks and pack it into vaults controlled by the BIS. From Vienna the gold was shipped to Switzerland.

On March 15, 1939, Hitler followed his storm troopers into Prague, Czechoslovakia. The directors of the Czech National Bank had been arrested and held at gunpoint, while their $48 million in gold reserves were demanded—gold that could not be found in the bank's vaults. The nervous bankers told Hitler that days earlier the BIS had instructed the Czech bank to forward the gold to the Bank of England. Montague Norman, governor Of the Bank of England and a rabid supporter of Hitler, had already made a paper transfer of the gold to Berlin, "for use in buying essential strategic materials toward a future war," reports Higham.

In April 1940, Hitler entered Belgium. The Belgian gold reserves Were shipped to the central bank in France, then transferred to the Reichsbank. From the Reichsbank the gold was shipped to the BIS. The gold reserves of every nation Hitler conquered (except those of France) were shipped to the BIS. When the Germans entered France in 1940, its gold reserve went untouched, since her central bank was a member of the BIS. Gold was taken only from those nations whose central banks were not members of the BIS.

In addition to pulling off the greatest gold heist in history, by 1942 the Gestapo had accumulated hundreds of chests of gold and jewels including monocles, spectacle frames, watches, cigarette cases, lighters, wedding rings, dentures, and teeth fillings taken from murdered concentration camp victims. The booty was melted down into gold bars weighing 20 kilograms each and deposited in the Reichsbank. In 1944 when Hitler realized that it was inevitable that Germany Would lose the war, he and his Nazi hierarchy began depositing the gold bars with the BIS. Later that year, at their fourth annual meeting since the beginning of the war, the American president of the BIS, CFR member Thomas H. McKittrick, and the polished British board members sat down with their enemies, the German, Japanese and Italian executive staff, to discuss what to do with the $378 million in gold that had been sent to the bank by the Nazi government for use by its leaders after the war."

The American Response

Meanwhile, Freemason Henry Morgenthau, the American secretary of the treasury from 1934 to 1945, began to distrust English Freemasonry's big money power. For example, he was aware that British bankers controlled the Bank for International Settlements. He also knew that the Nazis were using the BIS as a storehouse for their stolen loot, but publicly he said nothing about it. In fact, on March 26, 1943, Congress man Jerry Voorhis of California entered a resolution in the House Of Representatives calling for an investigation of the BIS. Morgenthau was interested, but being a Mason, would have no part in a public investigati01i of his English Masonic brothers.

Apparently Congress felt the same as Morgenthau, for at that time 54 percent of the Congress and 53 percent of the Senate were Masons. The resolution died in Congress. In January 1944, Congressman John M. Coffee introduced a similar resolution. Again, it was tabled.

In 1945 the BIS began assisting the Nazis by making "financial transactions that would help them dispose of their loot." The majority of the wealth was transferred to Argentina, where it has since been used to build up English Freemasonry's South American network of drug production and distribution (see chapter seven). Assisting English Freemasonry was the newly formed postwar Nazi International.

The Bretton Woods Plan

The British descendants of the Masons who stripped the assets of Imperial China were the same English Freemasons who confiscated the gold of American citizens during the Great Depression, and who plundered European gold reserves during World War Il. Now they planned to rob every nation in the world, including the United States, by stealing the gold reserves remaining at Fort Knox. Two additional post-war international central banks were created after World War II to accomplish this task. The Encyclopaedia Britannica relates the ostensible purpose of these two banks:

The governments of the Allied countries in the postwar world saw that the currency chaos and beggar-my-neighbour policies, of the 1930s must be avoided. First, the reconstruction of the world monetary system was needed, and the United Nations Monetary and Financial Conference held at Bretton Woods [New Hampshire] in July 1944 sought to do this through the establishment of the International Monetary Fund and the International Bank for Reconstruction and Development (or World Bank).

The Bretton Woods Conference was packed with British Masons, including John Maynard Keynes, Anthony Eden, and Bertrand Russell. American Masons were present as well, including Morgenthau. The remainder were members of the Council on Foreign Relations. The controversy over the murky transactions of the Bank for International Settlements was by then well-known and had to be dealt with first. Morgenthau, as a high degree

Mason and secretary of the treasury, led the charge, demanding that the BIS be quietly disbanded. CFR member Dean Acheson, along with CFR bankers Winthrop Aldrich and Edward E' Brown of the Chase (later Chase-Manhattan) and First National banks of New York, wanted it retained. Aldrich and Brown were supported by the Dutch delegation and by J.W. Beyen of Holland, the former president of the BIS. Leon Fraser of the First National Bank of New York also stood with them. So did the British delegation. English Freemason Keynes felt that the BIS should continue until a new world bank and an international monetary fund were set up in the soon-to-be established United Nations. Morgentlmau insisted the BIS must go and approved its disposal, but at the close or the Bretton Woods conference, the Bank for International Settlements was still in business. So it was that in those last months of World War II, gold stolen by the Nazis poured into the Swiss National Bank, was laundered, and transferred to the BIS to be used for another day.

International Monetary Fund

Before the Bretton Woods conference adjourned, the formation of the International Monetary Fund (IMF) was discussed, and a year later it was founded under the auspices of the United Nations. The same Anglophile central bank stockholders who controlled the majority of stock in the BIS and the Federal Reserve Bank, were also the major stockholders in the IMF. The purported purpose of the IMF was to loan money to underdeveloped Third World nations to finance industrial development—which, in fact, meant they were to produce cheap raw materials for rebuilding war-torn Europe and Japan. It was soon apparent that the developing nations could not stay solvent or pay off their ever increasing national debt without producing illegal drugs. According to Dr. John Coleman, a former British intelligence officer, London, even in the days which saw the rise of Hitler to power, saw that it would eventually need drug revenues from South America. Coleman reports:

> "In 1933 the British government had invested $7 billion dollars in land in South America that was only capable of

growing drugs. "After World War Il, even to our day, when South American nations are unable to pay their national debts to the IMF, millions of acres are leased to those governments by white-gloved Englishmen to grow "a more salable produce for export."

The Bretton Woods plan proposed to establish not only the IMF, but also another bank the International Bank for Reconstruction and Development—also known as the World Bank, to be headquartered in Washington, D.C. The World Bank would provide the war-torn nations of Europe and the Pacific rim with funds to purchase cheap raw materials from Third World nations financed by the IMF.

The Anglophile conspirators at Bretton Woods realized that the rapid expansion necessary to rebuild Europe was not possible unless world currency could be inflated as the dollar had been inflated in the United States during the Great Depression. By taking the world off gold convertible currency, the rapid expansion that was impossible after World War I, became possible after World War II. This expansion would require the confiscation of the world's gold, legally and voluntarily, of course, as had been done in the United States from 1933 to 1935.

International Currency?

Proposals for an international currency were also debated at the Bretton Woods Conference.

Freemason John Maynard Keynes argued for an international gold reserve deposited in a neutral country with international bank notes issued on the basis of this gold reserve. According to Keynes:

> "It is not necessary in order to attain these ends that we should dispossess gold from its traditional use. It is enough to supplement and regulate the total supply of gold and of the new money taken together. The new money must not be freely convertible into gold, for that would require that gold reserves

should be held against it, and we should be back where we were, but there is no reason why the new money should not be purchasable for gold."

The adopted plan called not for an international currency but for a mixture of domestic currencies from member nations. And it prohibited these currencies from being convertible to gold. It did, however, maintain the gold standard and permit a gold reserve to be held by the IMF. The gold reserve would be stocked from specified, but voluntary contributions from the gold reserves of each member nation. In addition, each member nation would voluntarily contribute a specified amount of its domestic currency.

Notice that these are "contributions" and not "loans." To implement an international monetary system of this kind, the problem of national sovereignty had to be overcome. Therefore, most of the conferees wanted to hatch the plan in secret because nations with gold reserves, if cognizant of what was happening, would be reluctant to give up any portion of those reserves to an international body. If shrouded in secrecy, however, the IMF plan would be sure to pass in every member nation's legislature because the majority of elected seats in these bodies were held either by Masons or members of the Council on Foreign Relations, all of whom had been schooled in globalism. Keynes argued that the system would not succeed if hatched in secret, but he was overruled.

European nations posed no problem to the conspirators because most of Europe's gold had been stolen by the Nazis during World War 11 and was already in their possession. But, what of American gold? "Two-thirds of the world's gold, worth $24 billion, was held in the United States at Fort Knox. And gold in the Second World of communist nations and the Third World of non-aligned, or underdeveloped nations was required. How could the IMF get these sovereign nations to give up their hordes of precious metals?

The Bretton Woods conspirators devised an elaborate scheme for this form of "legal" asset stripping. The plan called for the central banks in member nations of the United Nations to donate a percent of their assets in the IMF. Twenty-five percent of that donation was to come from each nation's .995 fine gold reserves, while 75 percent was to be in their own national currency. Following this initial donation, member nations were to contribute annually in the same percentages. The United States, of course, was to contribute the greatest amount.

The financial cost of this to the United States can be gauged from the following one-year contribution of U.S. funds to the IMF: The 1983 quota increase demanded of the United States by the IMF, and passed by an Anglophile dominated Senate, was $8.6 billion, substantially more than any other single nation's contribution. This is a contribution—nota loan, not an investment.

With these figures, how many annual contributions would it take to deplete the $24 billion of gold stock at Fort Knox. It took fourteen years, from 1945 to 1959, to liquidate the American gold reserves in this manner. Today there is n° 995 fine delivery gold in Fort Knox. According to the Encyclopaedia Britannica, good delivery gold was gone from Fort Knox by the end of the 1950s.

How was the gold spirited out of Fort Knox and out of our country? According to one soldier (a personal friend of the author), he and his Army Corp of Engineers stationed at Fort Knox during the 1950s were given orders to load the gold on milk trucks and transport it to the World Bank in Washington, D.C. From there it was shipped to Europe and Japan to rebuild those devastated nations. In 1941 our nation owned almost two-thirds of the world's good delivery gold stock; by the end of 1959, Europe had about twice the gold reserves as did the United States. Today the balance of gold stock at Fort Knox is "gold alloy" of fineness or less, mostly coin melt (i.e., from the coins seized by our Masonic President Franklin D. Roosevelt in 1933). This gold alloy stock is estimated to be valued at $2 billion and cannot be classified and sold as good delivery gold. Of course, this is only an estimate of U.S. gold reserves, for no inventory of our gold reserves has been taken since 1933. Although audits of the seals on vault doors were conducted in 1953 and 1976, audits of seals are not inventories of gold bars. We, while still a democratic people, should demand the seals be broken and a CNN televised inventory taken of our gold reserves. This inventory should be supervised by American citizens. And the gold should be tested by a independent laboratory for fineness. We will then know the truth that our nation has no fine delivery gold stocks.

Debtor Nations

We have seen how the Masonic BEIC merchants plundered China through "free trade" drug trafficking. Between 1829 and 1840, a total of seven million silver dollars entered China, while 56 million silver dollars were sucked out by the soaring opium trade. Such massive flight capital of precious metals made China a debtor nation.

In a different manner, but with identical results, the IMF has stripped the United States of its gold reserves, making it the largest debtor nation on earth. As of the writing of this book, the United States owes in excess of $4 trillion dollars to the Masonic world bankers, who control the central banks of the seven member nations of the Trilateral Commission. Should a nation borrowing from the IMF refuse to make payments on its national debt, it would be classified by the IMF as a loan risk. No central bank or world bank will loan money to a nation that is a loan risk. If funds are cut off, the government shuts down. The terrible fact is that as a nation, we are borrowing from our own contribution to the IMF and then paying interest on it to the Anglophile stockholders of the Federal Reserve and World Bank. This could only have been accomplished by globalist legislators, who view our sovereign nation as a threat to Freemasonry's long-desired world government.

Recession and Inflation

One of the problems with the Bretton Woods System of inflation is the time bomb of spiraling inflation it creates. Sooner or later the bubble will burst, and the Bretton Woods system will collapse. Several stopgap measures have therefore been taken to alleviate this problem. One of the means by which a nation's central bank controls inflation is through rising and falling interest rates. When inflation is high, interest rates are raised to stop spending. When spending slows, recession sets in and the banks lower interest rates to increase spending. This is what produces our roller coaster economy of growth versus recession.

Beginning in the mid-1960s, another problem faced the Bretton Woods system: the rapid growth of the space program and the arms race between the East and West was breaking the bank. In fact, there was not enough gold in the world to sustain such rapid expansion, which would have the same effect as spiraling inflation—the Bretton Woods System would collapse. To bring in revenue, English Freemasonry sent its rock and roll stars on world tours to increase the drug traffic (more on this in chapter 7). Although this brought desperately needed money into their banks, it also depleted their gold reserves even more, because the Oriental opium farmers demanded more gold bullion as they increased opium production. To prevent the impending financial disaster these problems posed, English Masonic operative and CFR member David Rockefeller founded the Trilateral Commission (TC) in 1973 to study the situation.

At the founding meeting, Triangle Paper 14, "Towards a Renovated International System," concluded that the 1944 Bretton Woods system had already "come under increasing strain," and events had forced traumatic changes. Part of the changes included the phasing out of the gold standard, which freed gold reserves for use in English Freemasonry's illegal drug trade. Two years earlier, a letter sent to Congressman J. Kenneth Robinson from Gene E. Godley, assistant secretary for legislative affairs at the treasury, illustrates the out-of-date views on gold held by the U.S. Treasury:

There is, moreover, a high degree of uncertainty about the usefulness of gold as money. Its monetary role has greatly diminished in recent years, and its market price has varied widely. Thus, our gold stocks no longer represent an assured source of financing for our imports.

This letter was written for congressional consumption. Congress was being prepared for what would come next: in 1971, the United States went off the gold standard. The wealthiest nation on earth had no more gold reserves to donate to the IMF; no more gold reserves to back its own currency. The Masonic bankers were forced to devise another plan to prop up the failing Bretton Woods system. We can only speculate what was discussed at the founding meeting of the Trilateral Commission. Well-seasoned in creating banking crises, the same British Masonic bankers who founded the Trilateral Commission (TC), also control the oil industry and could create a fuel crisis. As subsequent events suggest, in that meeting the conspirators planned to create such a crisis to inflate fuel prices. Immediately following the meeting, the world experienced its first fuel crisis, causing oil prices to triple. As a result, the rapidly escalating price of crude oil sent billions of dollars rushing through their faltering banks. This, however, was only another temporary fix. By 1978 the Bretton Woods system had totally collapsed. A second fuel crisis was created, but not in time to save the system.

That year conspiracy researchers had finally discovered what was going on. Antony Sutton and Patrick Wood, in Trilateral-s Over Washington (1978), reveal how the fuel crisis was created.

They document our abundant energy, which was kept under lock during the crisis. They show how the manipulators suppressed this information, and finally, they name who the creators of the crisis were. Not surprising, concluded Sutton and Wood, the crisis creators were individuals who owned both the oil companies and the banks. Moreover, the majority were members of the Trilateral

Commission. Sutton and Wood briefly explain the interlocking connection of these conspirators:

The tight interlock among the seven majors [oil companies] both with each other and the Commission makes for ready transference of Trilateral ideas and proposals; and oil company ideas and proposals are funneled through the TC and related "think tanks."

Sutton and Wood also concluded that "trilateralism is heavily interlocked with both energy companies and energy policy formation in the White House." Jimmy Carter, one of the sixty-five founding members of the Trilateral Commission, was in the White House. Statistics reveal that during Carter's tenure as president, illegal drug use doubled in America. Not until the Anglophile Clinton administration came to power did drug use double again. During the Carter administration, the dope economy became the stated, official policy of the IMF. The Masonic bankers once again escalated the sale of illegal drugs, as they had done in the 1960s, to build up the reserves of the IMF with drug money until a better solution could be found. By 1983, that better system was the euromarket. Headquartered in Lausanne, Switzerland, with branches in London, and various private islands, and subject to no scrutiny by national financial authorities, the Euromarket depends on a $300 billion per year (1985 figures) flow of money from illegal flight capital, evasion, narcotics, and other criminal activities to stay in business.

When the IMF decided to pump up the collapsing Bretton Woods system by laundering illegal drug money, the September 1978 issue of the Executive Intelligence Review published a Special Report on the World Bank and the IMF's deliberate promotion of the drug trade. The report exposed London and Wall Street policies that dictated Britain, Opium Wars in the last century, and which had now become the operant doctrine of the collapsing Bretton Woods system. "And behind it all", reported the EIR,

"was the chain of command which led up the ladder of the Scottish Rite to the top rung of English Freemasonry."

Setting the Price of Gold

The major portion of the world's confiscated gold is stored in underground bank vaults in Zurich, Switzerland. Most of what goes into circulation is shipped from Zurich to London to Hong Kong, because gold is the "universal currency for opium transshipped through Southern Iran.

For centuries, farmers of opium in the Orient have refused payment in anything other than gold or diamonds because they are the only stable means of exchange. Carol White, in The New Dark Ages Conspiracy, confirms that "diamonds serve as a medium of exchange at the top levels of the opium trade, and in normal periods of currency exchange, variations in gold and diamond prices are closely tied to fluctuations in the opium markets." This is why following the Opium Wars, South Africa and its surrounding colonized territories became so important to London.

English Masonic bankers needed the precious gems and metals of the region to finance their drug trade. The primary reason Great Britain fought the Boer Wars at the turn of the twentieth century was to control the diamond and gold fields. The man most responsible for these wars was English Freemason Cecil Rhodes of Rhodes Scholarship fame. As a colonist to South Africa, Rhodes was the primary force behind the creation of the British Commonwealth nations of South Mica and Rhodesia. And as a major partner in the DeBeers diamond mining company and Consolidated Goldfields, which he founded with Rothschild's financial backing, he was brought into the darker side of the Empire—the British opium trade from India and China.

The banks of Hong Kong have been the world's largest handlers of gold bullion and diamonds.

The mad Societies, with gold furnished by the Hong Kong banks, buy opium from the farmers of Southeast Asia and transport it to Hong Kong in exchange for more gold. Today the British

Masonic banking house of Rothschild controls the price of gold. Every morning at 10:30 a.m., five of the clan set the world price of gold bullion in the opulent Gold Room of N.M. Rothschild and Sons, in London, England. White confirms that the price set is tied to fluctuations in the opium markets.

The IMF and the Third World

Once the war-ravaged nations of Europe and the Pacific rim were rebuilt by loans from the World Bank, the IMF turned it sights to the nations of the Third World. When these nations gained their independence, central banks were established in them to handle the increased revenues generated by drug trafficking. We shall concentrate only on Central and South America, since these countries immediately affect the United States.

Before the South American nations were allowed to borrow from the IMF, they were required to adopt austerity programs. The BIF demanded that their governments

> "shut down capital-intensive industry, collapse 'inflationary' salary levels, force urban populations back to the county side, and maintain high interest rates, along with their promotion of tourism, casinos and other such 'services' which provide quick cash tot for debt payments."

As expected, the requirements of the austerity program shut down much normal revenue-generating businesses and created a desperate need for capital to pay off national debt—a debt which could be paid by revenues from drug production. In response to that need, the British government, which had in 1933 invested $7 billion in land south of our border—land useful for growing drugs only—leased millions of acres to grow "a more salable produce for export."

International bankers inside and out of the IMF confirm that IMF requirements in fact create debtor nations and then exploit them. Frederick Wills, the former Foreign Minister of Guyana, tells how the IMF operates within a debtor nation to force it, in effect, to grow drugs: The problem is that all these mechanisms (IMF austerity requirements for loan approval) aggravated the problem rather than solving it. For instance, the first thing they tell you is to devalue. Sometimes they used the word "devalue," sometimes they used the word "alignment," but they meant devaluation.

And that meant that imports became more expensive, which increased the debt, and it also meant that the debts increased automatically, because the value of your money depreciated. So the balance of payments deficit increased!

The difficulty was that the prices for your exports, which were largely raw materials and food, were not controlled by you. Except for oil, the commodity prices were always low, sometimes lower than the cost of production. This means that you never earned enough from your export receipts to cover your import bill. So structurally there was always a balance of payments deficit, which meant that you had to negotiate with the IMF because the banks told you that you couldn't get any loans or credits unless you got the seal of approval of the IMF.

So whether you wanted to or not, you dealt with the IMF. When you got there, you would get too little, too late. Secondly, their strategy was to make sure that you were in a worse condition after you joined than when you entered, because the IMF was formed to reconstruct the world as perceived by the Bretton Woods conferees. They required cheap raw materials for the processing economies of Western Europe. Therefore the recovery of Western Europe was premised on cheap raw material, so that you couldn't get increased prices for your raw materials.

The countries hope that, by getting the IMF seal of approval, this will open the gates for credit from other countries and private banks. But the IMF seal of approval requires successful acceptance of the IMF program. And since you didn't succeed, the flow of funds from money markets and banks is dried up. The government ministers started to think, "What export drive could we have which could realize a quick cash flow, to stem this balance of payments gap?"

There is only one commodity that satisfies that requirement: dope, heroin, marijuana.

In several countries officials from the IMF and the Bretton Woods system would come down and say "your future lies in agriculture." But in agriculture you have the following problems: High technology is expensive; that increases your import bill. So you have to use the "appropriate technology" that you do have, to produce those goods which can satisfy your local market and a bit for export. You cannot compete with the great agricultural countries like Argentina, Canada, the United States and Australia. Therefore, the kind of crop you have to produce for export has to be one in which you have the edge and they don't, and that's dope.

John Holdson, a senior official for Latin America in the World Bank's International Trade and Monetary Flows department, confirmed the universality of the IMF economic scenario: know the coca industry here is highly advantageous to producers. In fact, from their point of view, they simply couldn't find a better product. Its advantages are that no elaborate technology is required, no hybrid seeds, and land and climate are perfect." And an international banker in New York explained in 1978 why drugs were grown in South America as an export product: Coffee prices are simply too unstable, always fluctuating on the world Market...

Drugs, on the other hand, provide a stable source of income at all times... I happen to know that the World Bank has been pressuring some Latin American countries to find some way of statistically accounting for their contraband flows.

The INT, Drugs, and Offshore Banking

In March 1983, the Senate Permanent Investigations Subcommittee (SPIS) issued a report entitled, "Crime and Secrecy: The Use of Offshore Banks and Companies." The report, the outcome of a two-year study by the U.S. Senate, charged that the $1.7 trillion Euromarket system (the Bretton Woods replacement, also controlled by the IMF) is heavily dominated by narcotics traffickers, smugglers, and organized crime cartels which are financially looting the United States. The report documented how the international narcotics trade, the "biggest business in the world," was conducted through the secret electronic transfer of funds to Switzerland from offshore (meaning unregulated) banking centers.

One of the most devastating aspects of the SPIS investigation was the identification of the International Monetary Fund—the supranational agency allegedly created to help countries in financial straits as knowingly participating in the design of banking policies which promote the World narcotics trade. The evidence presented showed that from the 1960s, the IMF and the Bank of England have participated in, protected, encouraged, defended, and even helped run offshore banking centers. With the knowledge that many of these havens are in turn used as central Control points for the highest levels of the drug trade.

The SPIS report takes as its starting point the estimation by experts that the illegal drug economy in the United States ranges from $100 to $330 billion in flight capital (money that leaves the country) annually (1983 figures); or around ten percent of the total U.S. Gross National Product. The study also reports that London is the leading center worldwide for the concealment of these funds; and that two-fifths of all foreign banking activities out of Switzerland are performed in conjunction with other offshore centers. Switzerland is thus the center for the practice of what is called the "layering" of secret financial accounts so that the beneficiary is impossible to determine.

The SPIS task force also concluded (apart from the magnitude of the laundering operations), illegal financial operations are now so tightly interwoven with "legitimate" operations in the Euromarkets, that illegal funds constitute a threat to the stability of the world banking system.

For example, when you have crooks running a corrupt world banking system, it is inevitable that some of those crooks will steal from the system for their own personal gain. A chief example presented by the report was the 1982 bankruptcy of an offshore subsidiary of Banco Ambrosiano of Milan, Italy—a bank controlled by the secretive Propaganda-2 Masonic Lodge. The CEO of Banco Ambrosiano, Freemason Roberto Calvi, stole via electronic fund transfers $1.3 billion from various member banks of the Euromarkets and deposited the funds in his own private bank accounts scattered throughout South America. (This will be discussed fully in the next chapter.)

The report named the banks in the United States and Canada through which illegal drug money is laundered. They are Canada's Bank of Nova Scotia, Barclay's Bank, and offshore divisions of David Rockefeller's Chase Manhattan Bank. The CEOs of all these banks are also members of British Freemasonry's Council on Foreign Relations (CFR) and Trilateral Commission (TC).

The Euromarket

When the Senate's report on crime and offshore banking was sent to London to request "cooperation between the United States and Britain in dismantling criminal activities in offshore centers," British officials rejected, out-of-hand, the Senate Permanent Investigations subcommittee proposal for cooperation. The reason that no investigation will ensue from London is that IMF officials have in several cases actually been the authors of legislation creating these off-shore banking havens. The IMF offers outside consultant services to help countries set up Hong Kong-style "separate accounting books" for off-shore banking centers that want to appear legitimate. These activities are centered in the IMF's Central Banking Department, which worked closely with British financial officials during the 1970s to create central banking authorities in the Caribbean. According to IMF officials, several Caribbean countries with whom they have worked are known to openly encourage narcotics and other illegal financial flows because they make good business sense. The lucrative business of drug trafficking is precisely what the

International Monetary Fund had in mind when they helped establish off-shore banking centers. The *London Observer* wrote a few months later:

> "In the complicated and topsy-turvey world of international finance the International Monetary Fund is now effectively helping those who want to legalize pot."

Two years following the SPIS report, the Bank for International settlements (BIS) in its 1985 annual report bragged about its success in stripping the world's assets. Apparently, English Freemasonry is now confident that it cannot be stopped in forcing on the world its long awaited universal monetary system—the Euromarket.

These designs were further confirmed when the Masonic oligarchy, for whom the BIS serves as an enforcement agency, met in Hong Kong on June 4, 1985, for its annual deliberation. In that meeting, according Switzerland's most powerful banker, Freemason Rainer E. Gut of the giant Credit Suisse, the British Masonic banking fraternity plans the demolition of all national supervision of national credit markets, and the final integration of all national credit markets into the so-called international "Euromarket."

The Euromarket, based in Switzerland, London, and various private islands, and subject to no scrutiny by national financial author-ides, depends on a $300 billion per year flow of money from illegal flight capital, tax-evasion, narcotics, and other criminal activities, to stay in business. The next chapter will document how these criminal activities are conducted through Masonic Lodges in Italy and South America.

Chapter 6

A FREEMASONRY OF TERRORISTS

Terrorists are very difficult, if not impossible, to control unless they happen to be fanatically committed to some higher authority… The signs are that the German, French, Italian, and Belgian groups may be creating a freemasonry of terrorists.

The New Yorker, July 8, 1985

B eginning in the mid-1970s and continuing through the mid-1980s, the assassinations of European politicians, judges, and bankers by so called terrorists, the mysterious death of one pope, and the attempted assassination of another put Europeans in a quandary. It was not surprising to learn that the "terrorists" were traced to organized crime. The links between the Red Brigades (and other terrorist organizations), and the Mafia are well-documented.

What was shocking to hear—at least to Americans—was a belated report in 1988 by the American news media confirming what the Europeans had known since 1980—that European "terrorists" did not always take their orders from the Mafia, but from a Masonic Lodge called Propaganda Duo, or P-2 Freemasonry. The Italian government, for example, had by 1981 uncovered a plot by an Italian terrorist named Pagliai, who was paid $2 million for planned assassinations. The money was traced to banks in Argentina controlled by P-2 Freemasonry.

Pagliai, a member of the Red Brigades, was extradited to Italy where he was charged for the 1980 Bologna train station bombing. In May 1980 a member of the Red Brigades, Marco

Affatigato, told a Genoese newspaper that the P-2 Lodge financed the Red Brigades to kidnap and ritually murder Italian Prime Minister Aldo Moro in 1978. The P-2 Lodge was also heavily involved in multi-billion dollar drug-for-weapons deals with the Ayatollah Khomeini's Iran'.

P-2 Freemasonry, which specializes in drug trafficking and money laundering, is patterned after Joseph Mazzini's revolutionary Propaganda Uno (P-1) Masonic Lodges of a century ago. Of course, the American news media, which has largely been under Masonic control for nearly a century, discounted the significance of the P-2 Lodge by stating that it is not "regular Masonry."

Meanwhile, The New Yorker, in an attempt to make some sense out Of why European governments were unable to stop a decade of terror, could only explain that the clandestine assassins were a "freemasonry of terrorists." The magazine was aware that Western European terrorists were not backed by the former Soviet Union, which had in the past employed the downtrodden and poor to execute its state-sponsored terrorism. Not so in Western Europe, said The New Yorker:

Among the European countries, Italy harbors the richest variety of terrorist groups... In Rome, they are mostly from the upper class... And some university professors are terrorist leaders. Giovanni Senzani, the last leader of the Red Brigades, was a professor... In France and Germany, terrorism is still elitist.

These are all people selected to perform bold missions. They are a continuum of cellular units. There may be a brain a clever brain—behind it, but the whole is animated by religious passion... Neither the [formerl Soviet Union nor any of its client states supports the terrorists in Western Europe.

Little did The New Yorker know (or maybe it was not telling) that the "clever brain" behind these European "terrorists" was Freemasonry. In fact, the terrorism afflicting Europe was a continuation of the war between English Grand Lodge Freemasonry and French Grand Orient Freemasonry.

Terrorists or Masons?

Ritual murderers kill passionately; they also document the murder in a grotesque way such as by carving symbols into the flesh of the victim's body, or by painting symbols on walls surrounding the scene of the murder, usually with the blood of the victim. These symbols are intended to tell a story about the murderer, the murdered, and the satanic organization by which the murder was ordered and/or performed. For example, if the murder is committed or ordered by Freemasonry, Masonic symbols are left at the scene for the following reasons: (1) to show the hierarchy in Freemasonry that this was a Masonic murder; (2) to warn all Masons to follow the Masonic code of silence, or suffer a like fate; (3) to document the ritual nature of the murder for completing initiation into a higher Masonic degree; or (4) to prove to the Masonic paymaster that the hit man accomplished his task.

Terrorists, who murder indiscriminately, kill for a different reason. They desire to bring worldwide attention to their cause, or hope to polarize a government to gain concessions for their ideology. They may be controlled by a state, a radical group, or a secret society such as Freemasonry.

The word "terrorist" is a relatively new word, coined in 1795 following the French Revolution.

Before that date, terrorists were known in France as Jacobins because of their membership in the Jacobin Clubs. Volume one of Scarlet and the Beast has shown how the Jacobin Clubs were controlled by Grand Orient Freemasonry. In 1793 the Jacobins brought to old France a blood bath so horrific that history records it as the "Reign of Terror."

The Post-War Masonic International

A hundred years later, terrorists were called anarchists, nihilists, and communists. Again, we have shown that all these groups were controlled by the resident Masonic Lodges within the nations from which they operated. Most members of these groups also belonged to Joseph Mazzini and Henry Palmerston's Masonic youth organization "Young Europe". Mazzini's mobsters did not consider themselves lawbreakers but rather political activists, working to win political freedoms by overthrowing monarchies and establishing in their place democratic republics. The New Yorker confirms that terrorists still see themselves not as outlaws or criminals but as political activists:

Terrorists naturally think of themselves not as criminals or enemies of society but as political activists, and numerous Europeans have tended to accept at least some of them at their Own evaluation. In 1981, the incoming government of France's President Francois Mitterrand granted amnesty to the two leaders of Direct Action, an organization that seemed less threatening than the claims it made for itself; but now Direct Action is a full-blown terrorist group, with fraternal links to more experienced groups, such as Germany's Red Army Faction … and Italy's Red Brigades.

Why Would Mitterrand grant amnesty to terrorists? The answer is simply that he and his government are controlled by the same Freemasonry that controls the terrorists the Grand Orient. The leadership of the Socialist party (Mitterrand's party), for example, as a whole overlaps extensively with the membership of the Grand Orient Lodge, Which oversees the "libertarian" projects of the party. Mitterrand, a 33rd degree Freemason, is also a member of the Grande Loge National de France the only Scottish Rite Lodge recognized by the Grand Mother Lodge Of England.

The New Yorker's next statement reveals that its editors were aware of but not forthright in naming Freemasonry as the "clever brain" behind European terrorism. They noted that "the right to asylum is a French tradition dating from the revolution of 1789; it was written into the constitution of the Fourth and Fifth Republics, and the Third Republic made the country a sanctuary for the anti-Fascist enemies of Mussolini and Franco." We have already documented in volume one that all of France's republics were controlled by Freemasonry, beginning with the first in 1789. The New Yorker, however, stopped short of telling us that tie anti-Fascist enemies of Mussolini harbored in France during the Third Republic were none other than the Masons that Mussolini exiled from Italy in 1925. In fact, during World War II, Mussolini and Hitler together nearly destroyed Continental Freemasonry.

After World War Il, the Allied Powers rehabilitated Freemasonry in Italy. It was this post-war Italian Grand Orient Lodge that organized the P-2 Lodge in 1966. And P-2 Freemasonry controls Western European and Latin American terrorism. Behind P-2 (initially at least) stood the corrupt London and Swiss Euromarket banking establishment, via the Grand Mother Lodge of the City of London. Within this control structure, the following elements overlap: "certain oligarchical families (particularly in Italy, Switzerland, and Great Britain); their associated financial institutions; elements of various Eastern and Western intelligence services; secret conspiratorial societies, particularly of Freemasonic and other pseudo-religious stripes; the international organized crime network; and the still-extant 'Nazi International'.

The Murder of Roberto Calvi

For the first time in post-war history, this Masonic control structure was exposed to public scrutiny in the summer of 1982 in connection with the scandal surrounding the P-2 Lodge. The scandal, which included the Masonic ritual murder of Roberto Calvi, a well-known Italian banker and member of P-2, was just another conflict between English Grand Lodge and French Grand Orient Freemasonry. The investigations, of which there were many, revealed that Calvi's death was a Masonic ritual murder ordered by the British Brotherhood, who had accused him of treason.

London had hired Calvi to set up offshore banks and shell companies to launder Mafia drug money before it could be safely deposited in London's Masonic banks. On June 17, 1982, Calvi was found hanging from Blackfriar's Bridge in the city of London. Proofs that the death of calvi was an English Grand Lodge ritual murder are many. We will list four: (I) he was killed in London; (2) Blackfriar was the name of the Grand Orient Lodge in Italy to which Calvi belonged; (3) around Calvi's neck was a Masonic cable tow, indicating that he was led to the scene of the murder by higher degree Masons; and (4) in his pockets were masonry bricks.

David A. Yallop, author of *In God's Name* (1984), confirms how deeply involved Calvi was in P-2 Freemasonry. According to Yallop, Calvi's responsibility was to launder Mafia drug money through the Vatican Bank for deposit in British Masonic banks. His contact was Bishop Paul Marcinkus, president of the Vatican Bank. In the fall of 1978, the first Pope John Paul discovered that the Vatican Bank was being used to launder drug money, and that some twenty-two bishops and cardinals were involved in the scheme. This pope made a decision to dismiss these prelates from service to the Church. On September 28, 1978, the pope retired for the evening, never to awaken again in this world. He had been on Peter's throne for only thirty-three days.

All the signs surrounding John Paul's death point to a Masonic ritual murder. First, he was about to release twenty-two of his prelates who had joined hands with Freemasonry. Second, he would have dismantled a multi-billion-dollar Masonic drug-related, money-laundering scheme operating out of the Vatican Bank. Third, he died in bed thirty-three days after he had become pope (the number 33 is a Masonic signature). Fourth, he was poisoned by an overdose of digitalis, a drug developed by French Grand Orient Freemasonry during the mid-eighteenth century to disguise an assassination as a heart attack.

Grand Orient Freemason Roberto Calvi, the man who set up the Vatican Bank money-laundering scheme, was most likely the Mason who gave the Order to poison the pope. Other money laundering banks and shell corporations throughout Central and South America bore Calvi's stamp. By way of his secret meetings, foreign associates, and dummy companies, Calvi could make dirty money disappear like aircraft in the Bermuda Triangle, then reappear in London's Masonic banks squeaky clean. In his multi-million-dollar transfers of money, he would use the Rothschild banks in Zurich, Switzerland, and in Guernsey, England, as well as the National Bank of Paris in Panama through P-2 shell corporations, such as Bellatrix in Panama. Calvi was not only successful because of his affiliation with P-2, he was one of the most brilliant scoundrels of all time. What brought about his Masonic ritual murder on June 17, 1982 is that he bilked his London masters of $1.3 billion to fund a secret project in South America on behalf of Grand Orient Freemasonry. As warning to Calvi's Grand Orient masters, the English Grand Lodge lured Calvi to London (the significance of the cable-tow around Calvi's neck) where he was ritually hanged on Blackfriar's bridge.

There is a limit to what a man can hide. Serving two masters is impossible. When Calvi was caught, he was murdered in clever Masonic fashion to send a message to other Masons who would dare steal from their fraternity brothers. The murders of Calvi and the pope were only two of many so-called terrorist hits that rocked Europe for a decade. In truth these "random" killings were not acts of terrorism but were Masonic ritual murders.

The War Between English and French Freemasonry

Money determines power, and English Freemasonry controls the money of the world. French Freemasonry, on the other hand, has been financially destitute from its inception. Consequently, in 1889 it was forced to bow to its British superior. From that date we can observe a shift in the headquarters of political conspiracy from Paris to London.

World War I was a last ditch effort by French Freemasonry to wrest political power from English Freemasonry. In that war the

Continental Brotherhood successfully took over Russia, established the Soviet Union, founded the League of Nations, and began a drive to use the USSR to communize all Europe and ultimately the world.

English Freemasonry, however, would not be outdone. World War I made her more wealthy and enabled London to fund the rise of Hitler for the purpose of destroying French Freemasonry's scheme. The result was World War Il, which war brought into the vaults of the British Masonic banks all the gold reserves on the Continent gold that Hitler had looted from each nation he conquered. Prior to World War II, English Freemasonry took political control of the United States of America through its subversive Council of Foreign Relations (CFR). During the war, the CFR planned, organized, and founded the United Nations. Following the war, French Freemasonry once again was forced to bow to its British superiors. In so doing, both Masonic powers agreed to cooperate in the U.N. Each, however, still tries to dominate the other. Hence in 1966, French Freemasonry founded the P-2 Lodge to wrest away from English Freemasonry its control of the lucrative drug trade.

The Plan: Co-opting the CIA and FBI

In 1860, 33rd degree Italian Grand Orient Freemason Joseph Mazzini, and his band of Masonic revolutionaries, lost their bid to unite Italy under a republic. English Freemasonry came to their aid by way of the British Navy to assist 33rd degree Grand Orient Freemason General Giuseppe Garibaldi in conquering the island or Sicily to create a homeland for Mazzini and his gang.

From this island hub, heroin from the Orient was distributed to the west by Mazzini's Mafia in behalf of English Grand Lodge Freemasonry. To protect the drug traffickers, Mazzini established a peculiar type of Grand Orient Lodge, and established many of them throughout Europe and South America. He named these lodges Propaganda Uno (P-1), and they fell under the authority of Italian Grand Orient Freemasonry. After the two World Wars, P-

1 lodges became obsolete when the Mafia and its drug trafficking came under the protection of both the CIA and the FBI.

Although it is hard to believe that our CIA and FBI would work with drug traffickers, we must understand that these institutions considered their decision to do so patriotic. After World War I, the greatest fear of Western intelligence was not organized crime, but communism. In fact, the West faced a crisis because by 1935 the communists had taken over three large trade unions in America. At any moment they could call a nationwide strike, which would devastate our economy at a time when we were just coming out of the Great Depression. After World War II, the communist crisis compelled the CIA to locate, shelter, and employ ex-Nazis to combat the spread of communism. In the same enterprise and for the same reasons, the FBI approached the Mafia for its assistance. J. Edgar Hoover, a 33rd degree Mason, made the initial contact with New York mob boss Frank Costello. In this secret meeting both men agreed that the Mafia would be permitted to take over the trade unions in order to keep the communists out. Beginning with this "patriotic" meeting, Hoover closed his eyes to the activities of organized crime in America.

The CIA was founded in 1947, and it handled the ex-Nazis. But the CIA's connection with the Nazis begins earlier, in 1944, when Hitler realized it was inevitable that Germany would lose the war. Hitler and his Nazi hierarchy began depositing Germany's gold reserves with the Bank for International Settlements, founded and controlled by the Masonic banking hierarchy in London.

The total deposit was $378 million in gold to be used by the Nazis after the war. In 1945 the BIS began assisting the Nazis by making financial transactions to dispose of their Wealth. The majority of the wealth was transferred to Argentina, where it has since been used to build up English Freemasonry's South American network of drug production and distribution. Assisting English Freemasonry was the newly formed, post-war Nazi International.

Near war's end, the Dulles Brothers, John and Allen (who was destined to head the CIA in 1953), both members of the Anglophile Council on Foreign Relations (CFR), advised London and Wall Street to leave the Nazi-Swiss headquarters untouched, along with the funds they had squirreled away there. The British government, as early as 1933, had already invested $7 billion in land in South America that was only good for growing drugs. By the end of the war, the British had already determined who among the Nazis would be spirited off to South America to manage this huge investment; the remnants of this investment are the South American drug cartels.

Meanwhile, in Switzerland former Nazis were attached to the Swiss Grand Lodge of Freemasonry headquartered in Lausanne, causing the editors of World Intelligence Review to comment in 1989 that "Lausanne is the home of the satanist core of Freemasonry, and some of the worst crimes against humanity were hatched in that city." Lausanne, for example, is headquarters for the corrupt Euromarket Masonic banks that handled the funds for P-2, which financed the three European rightwing terrorist organizations of the mid-1970s and 1980s mentioned earlier.

Moreover, descendants of the post-war Nazis, and those individuals who operate the Euromarkets, belong to the same Swiss Grand Lodge. The corrupt Euromarket banks hold the wealth of these neo-Nazis, giving them command of an extensive financial apparatus, which initially was fed by the wealth amassed by the Third Reich, and which is now funded by the neo-Nazis' illegal drug traffic in South America.

The Assassination of John F. Kennedy

After World War II, the ex-Nazis in South America established a network of Masonic lodges that extended from Argentina north to Cuba. These lodges operated as an "underground railroad" of protection as drugs were moved north. The final destination was Cuba, which was the North American hub for distribution of South American drugs in the United States. Freemason Fulgencio

Batista, the Cuban dictator, with the Mafia, controlled this small Caribbean island until Fidel Castro toppled Batista in 1958. On January 1, 1959, Castro took charge of Cuba, kicked out the Mafia and shut down the Western Hemisphere's largest distribution depot for South American drugs. With the loss of Cuba, the ex-Nazis contacted their friend Allen Dulles, been head of the CIA since 1953, and pressured him to rid of Castro. During the latter months of the Eisenhower administration, Dulles put together the strategy for the CIA-backed Bay of Pigs invasion scheduled for April 17, 1961. Meanwhile, John Kennedy, and not the Eisenhower-groomed Nixon, was elected as the thirty-fifth president of the United States. Kennedy's entire political career had been a war against the Mafia. He considered the Mob's exile from Cuba a victory, and saw the Bay of Pigs as a threat to his ultimate goal of destroyng the Mafia. Kennedy, therefore, pulled the plug on air support promised by the CIA for the Bay of Pigs operation; Castro remained in war. Kennedy furthermore planned to splinter the CIA into a thousand pieces and fire FBI Director J. Edgar Hoover, a 33rd degree Mason. The CIA, FBI, the Mafia, and the South American Nazi drug cartels, not to mention the controller of this apparatus, English Freemasonry, were livid. Together they planned the assassination of Kennedy.

The Assassination Cover-up

Garrison, the New Orleans attorney who brought the only case of conspiracy charges against a defendant for the murder of John F. Kennedy, implicated both the CIA and the Nazis in the assassination plot, but he failed to mention the Mafia or English Freemasonry. The thesis of David E. Scheim's book on the assassination is revealed by its title: Contract America: The Mafia Murder of President John F. Kennedy (1989). David S. Lifton, in Best Evidence: Disguise and Deception in the Assassination of John F. Kennedy (1988), shows how deeply involved the CIA was in the plot. He leaves no doubt that the CIA covered up both the plot to kill the president and the alteration of the president's body after the assassination. Lifton's book reproduces photographs of Kennedy's corpse; it is of interest to compare the photos on pages 586 and 587.

One picture shows the president's throat, which appears to have been slashed from left to right in true Masonic fashion as described in the oath of the initiation rites taken by the first degree Entered Apprentice. The oath reads, "binding myself under a no less penalty than that of having my throat cut across..."

The most damning evidence for the CIA's complicity in the murder is Presented in the recent book First Hand Knowledge: How I Participated in the CIA-Mafia Murder of President Kennedy (1992) by Robert D. Morrow. Morrow claims that he, on CIA orders, was the one who purchased the three rifles that killed JFK. He further alleges that J. Edgar Hoover and Richard Nixon knew of the plot, and that the government closed its eyes to the assassination plans. He says that Vice President Lyndon Johnson was told by Hoover that Kennedy had to be killed because he had de-escalated the Vietnam War a CIA war fought over the control of the illegal drugs in Southeast Asia. (The Vietnam War was resumed by President Johnson one day after the assassination.) Finally, Morrow describes how those involved in the conspiracy were deliberately and systematically executed. The FBI was also involved in the cover-up. Hoover allegedly recruited a band of killers from the "boss of bosses"—Mob chieftain Frank Costello. According to Michael Milan (pseudonym), author of The Squad (1989), Hoover ordered Milan, and two other hit men, to Kill "embarrassing" witnesses to the Kennedy assassination.

Far from revealing the truth of the Kennedy assassination, the Warren Commission continued the cover-up. Dr. John Coleman, a former British intelligence agent and author of Secrets of the Kennedy Assassination Revealed (1990), bluntly says that in fact the "Warren Commission was a Masonic-ordered cover-up." He points out that the late Earl Warren was a 33rd degree Mason, as is Gerald Ford, who was Warren's fellow commissioner. Against all expert evidence to the contrary, "it was Ford," says Coleman, "who invented the one-bullet theory. It was Gerald Ford ... who insisted that the experts who picked up the rifle had made a mistake in identifying it as a Mauser. It was Ford who said the doctors and nurses at Parkland Hospital in Dallas were mistaken about the wounds to President Kennedy's head."

Former CIA director and CFR member Allen Dulles also served on the Warren Commission and was complicitous in the cover-up.

Author David Scheim shows that "through-out the Commission meetings, Dulles concealed his knowledge of relevant CIA-Mafia assassination plots against Castro...

A major factor or probable cause of the plan to kill President Kennedy is revealed by Dr. Coleman, who notes that "one aspect of the Kennedy murder is never mentioned in any of the foregoing." Kennedy was ridding his administration of all the appointed bureaucrats who were either Masons or members of the Council on Foreign Relations (CFR). Coleman suggests that English Freemasonry was behind the plot to kill Kennedy' because Kennedy "desired to buck the British ... control of the White House..."

Italian Grand Orient Freemasonry, feeling the heat of the investigation into the Kennedy assassination, severed its relationship with the CLA and the FBI, and in 1966 organized P-2 Freemasonry to protect its drug traffickers. And like Mazzini's P-1 Lodges, P-2 also had its assassins do away with those who would either impede, or expose its operations. This new generation of Propaganda Lodges not only protected drug traffickers, they also developed a Grand Orient Masonic banking empire to compete with British Masonic bankers. Their scheme almost succeeded.

The Resurrection of Propaganda Lodges

Stephen Knight, a British investigative journalist, informs us in The Brotherhood: The Secret World of the Freemasons (1984), of how P-2 Freemasonry got its start: P-2 was formed in 1966 at the behest of the then Grand Master of the Grand Orient of Italy, Giordano Gamberini. The Grand Master's plan was to establish a group of eminent men who would be sympathetic and useful to Freemasonry. The man chosen to create this elite band was a rich textile manufacturer from the town of Arezzo in Tuscany. He had entered Masonry two years before and had risen to the Italian equivalent of Master Mason. His name was Licio Gelli.

Licio Gelli had joined a conventional Grand Orient lodge in November 1963. He rapidly rose to the position of Master Mason, which made him eligible to lead a lodge. His competence came to the attention of Gamberini, who assigned Gelli the task of resurrecting Propaganda lodges. Gelli, however, had ambitions for P-2 which Gamberini had never so much as imagined.

Gelli's ex-Nazis and his South American Drug Cartels

The origins of Gelli's plans for Propaganda-Duo (P-2) reach all the way back to the beginnings of the Spanish Civil War. In 1930 the Spanish Communist Revolution began, but not being well-organized, it faltered. Russian dictator Joseph Stalin sent "technicians" to Spain to assist in the revolution. All were bloodthirsty Grand Orient Masons who had participated in the indiscriminate slaughter of Russians during the Bolshevik Revolution. Upon arriving in Spain, they made contact with brother Masons, who offered them haven within the protected walls of the Spanish Grand Orient Lodges to plan their strategy. The Spanish Revolution proceeded in the same way as the Bolshevik Revolution—by the mass slaughter of Spanish citizens. Through these brutal means, the faltering Spanish Grand Orient revolution was strengthened.

The Spanish Civil War, 1937 to 1939, began as General Francisco Franco retaliated against the communists for the bloody revolution. Fighting alongside of Franco was the young Licio Gelli.

Gelli had witnessed the brutality of the Masons, and he developed an inveterate hatred of all things Masonic. Later he became a passionate supporter of Mussolini in the Duce's drive to annihilate Freemasonry from Italy and her colonies.

During World War II, Gelli became a Nazi SS-liaison officer in Italy. In 1943, when Nazi Germany SS officers realized that the Third Reich would fall, they planned their escape to a new homeland in South America, Gelli was there to assist them. Argentinean Juan Peron, an ambitious army colonel who took power there before the war ended, was a Nazi sympathizer. Martin Bormann, Hitler's secretary, began shipping millions of dollars from the Berlin Reichsbank in armored trucks to ports in southern Spain, where German U-boats transported it to Argentina. Despite the official neutrality of his country, Peron made certain that Bormann's treasure was kept in a safe place. In 1946, after Peron was elected president, the Nazis in Argentina were guaranteed protection. A United States report stated in 1945: "Nazi leaders, groups, and organizations have combined with Argentine totalitarian groups to create a Nazi-Fascist state."

In 1947 the CIA paid Licio Gelli to spirit away to South America the remaining members of the SS who were not useful for intelligence gathering against the USSR. Later, Gelli himself fled to Argentina, where he planned to turn that nation into a Western Hong Kong in competition with British bankers. Gelli held dual citizenship in Argentina and Italy, and was appointed an economic adviser in Italy. In 1963, Gelli returned to Italy to join Italian Freemasonry, the same Freemasonry that his beloved Mussolini so hated.

A paradox? Not at all. Gelli had developed his own strategy for the destruction of Freemasonry.

Where he differed with Mussolini was in how to do the job. Mussolini ruthlessly persecuted Masons. Gelli would take over from within. Yallop notes that, "ever anxious to increase his circle of power and influence, Gelli saw the [post-warl rehabilitated Masonic movement as the perfect vehicle." Gelli had long played the double-agent. Under Mussolini, he naturally hated communism as much as he did Freemasonry, since the former had developed from the later.

But, to destroy communism, one had to join the movement in order to learn its secrets. Gelli allowed himself to be recruited as a KGB agent, and during and after the war, he spied for the Communists. He logged everything he discovered about their movement and plans to be used against them at a later date. He planned to succeed where his friend Mussolini had failed.

In 1963, Gelli employed the same tactic by joining Grand Orient Freemasonry. He would use this cover to hide his plans from the British Masonic bankers. In 1966, he founded P-2, which while operating under the auspices of the Grand Orient, was directly controlled by Gelli. Gelli was able to recruit the top men or the world to his P-2 Lodge. In America, he initiated into P-2 two high officials, Henry Kissinger and Alexander Haig, both 32nd degree Scottish Rite Masons. Through their assistance, Gelli dined with Presidents Nixon, Carter, and Reagan, and many less important decision-makers in America. In Italy, Gelli had his Freemasons in every decision-making center in Italian politics, and was able to exert significant influence over those decisions… Nothing of vital importance had occurred in Italy in recent years which Gelli had not known about in advance or shortly after.

Gelli organized P-2 according to a similar structure employed by Weishaupt's Illuminati. The 953 men on its membership list, which published by the Italian government in the late spring of 1982,

> "were divided into seventeen groupings, or cells, each having its own leader. P-2 was so secret and so expertly run by Gelli that even its own members did not know who belonged to it.

Those who knew most were the seventeen cell leaders and they knew only their own grouping. Not even Spartaco Mennini, the then Grand Secretary of the Grand Orient of Italy, knew the entire membership of the Lodge. Only Licio Gelli knew that."

Gelli made sure that the Italian Communist party had no links with P-2. He had long since gathered all the information he needed to use against those involved in the Communist party.

To assure his success, he used blackmail as a trump card, and he used this unashamedly against all, even those in his own P-2 Lodge. Yallop wrote that

"in Gelli's blackmail file he had information on this banker, a secret dossier on that politician—his network spread from Argentina into Paraguay, into Brazil, Bolivia, Colombia, Venezuela, and Nicaragua."

At Licio Gelli's right hand was the sinister, yet brilliant banker, Roberto Calvi. Gelli found in Calvi a greedy little man through whom he could capture the banking business and drug trade from the British—at least in Italy and South America. Calvi was destined to become the "paymaster" of P-2.

Roberto Calvi: God's Banker

Roberto Calvi was born in Milan, Italy, in 1920. He fought for Mussolini on the Russian front in the Second World War. In 1947, Calvi followed his father into banking and went to work for Banco Ambrosiano in Milan. In 1963, three years before he met Gelli, Calvi struck a deal with English Masonic bankers to set up shell companies through which he would launder Mafia drug money for deposit in their banks. His first shell company was organized in 1963 in Luxembourg, and was called Compendium. In 1966, after meeting Gelli, Calvi joined P-2 Freemasonry. In 1971, Gelli introduced Calvi to Bishop Paul Marcinkus, president the Vatican bank. Calvi instantly became one of the select Vatican clan of "men of trust".

In 1971, Calvi also became managing director of Banco Ambrosiano. He changed the name of his Luxembourg shell company from Compendium to Banco Ambrosiano Holdings, and immediately began siphoning money from his bank to his shell company. Gelli would later use this knowledge to blackmail Calvi into funding his South American Operation.

Calvi established several offshore banks for the British under the Banco Ambrosiano name.

Bishop Marcinkus was on the board of one of these banks. Calvi soon struck a deal with Marcinkus to use the Vatican Bank to launder drug money for the Mafia. Until his death in 1982, Calvi was involved in a maze of dishonest transactions. Yallop observes of Calvi: His ability to dream up crooked schemes for laundering Mafia money, exporting lire illegally, evading taxes, concealing the criminal acts of buying shares in his own bank, rigging the Milan Stock Exchange, for bribery, for corruption, for perverting the course of justice, arranging a wrongful arrest here, a murder there—his ability to do all of this and more puts the Knight [as he was affectionately called] in a very special criminal class.

Roberto Calvi, "The Knight" was also known as "God's Banker" because of his affiliation with the Vatican Bank. Banco Ambrosiano of Milan and the Vatican Bank were so interlocked that the profits that were being channeled into the coffers of the Vatican Bank grew proportionately with Calvi's empire. Until his death, Calvi laundered money for the Mafia and P-2 on behalf of English Masonic bankers. Yallop informs us:

These functions were carried out with the assistance of the Vatican Bank, with money moving from Banco Ambrosiano into a Vatican account in Italy, then on to Banca del Gottardo or Union de Banques Suisse (UBS) in Switzerland. He laundered money from kidnappings, drug sales, arms deals, bank raids, holdups and thefts of jewelry and works of art. His criminal contacts ran the gamut, including what is sometimes known as High Mafia, ordinary run-of-the-mill murderers and members of right-wing terrorist organizations.

The reason that Calvi was able to break the law again and again with impunity was because the Vatican Bank operated as an offshore bank. By international law, it could not be audited by Italian banking authorities. It belonged to Vatican City, which functioned as a separate nation.

"With the close and continuous cooperation of the Vatican Bank," Yallop says "Calvi was able to dance an illegal and criminal path through the Italian laws again."

Calvi was successful at his game until the death of Pope Paul VI in 1978. The new pope, Albino Luciani (Pope John Paul I), had read in an Italian newspaper a list of 121 Masons who belonged to a lodge by the name of "The Great Vatican Lodge." In that list were cardinals, bishops, and high-ranking prelates—twenty-two in all. Among them were his secretary of state, Cardinal Villot, who had been a Mason since 1966. Also included were his foreign minister, Monsignor Agostino Casaroli; the Cardinal Vicar of Rome, Ugo Poletti; and Cardinal Baggio, Bishop I Paul Marcinkus, and Monsignor Donato de Bonis of the Vatican Bank. All were Freemasons. Even Pope Paul's secretary was a Mason. Luciani asked Cardinal Pericle Felici: "Did Pope Paul envisage a change in the Church's position on Freemasonry?"

Pope John Paul I intended to replace these traitors with men he could trust. He died in his sleep after thirty-three days in office. The new pope, Cardinal Karol Wojtyla of Poland (Pope John Paul II), promoted Paul Marcinkus to archbishop and allowed him to continue as head of the Vatican Bank. He also permitted Calvi to continue his activity through the Vatican Bank, so long as Calvi would financially assist Polish Solidarity against the Communists. "The total amount that was secretly and illegally funneled on behalf of the Vatican to Solidarity was over $100 million," says Yallop. In total, Marcinkus helped Roberto Calvi bilk the Banco Ambrosiano of $400 million dollars.

Through these illegal transfers of money, Calvi funded all of Licio Celli's South American operation. Meanwhile, Gelli set up a chain of P2 Masonic Lodges that stretched from Argentina to

Mexico. (Why Mexico was chosen by Gelli will be explained later.) Through these lodges, drugs were delivered to North America, where sixty percent of the world's illegal drugs are consumed.

With assistance from the 953 P-2 Masons in Europe and in North and South America, Gelli began developing his plan to go into offshore banking competition against English Freemasonry's Hong Kong banks.

When the P-2 scandal broke in Italy following the murder of Calvi in the summer of 1982, P-2 operatives in South America began to run for their lives. A few press agencies picked up on the stories. The Caracas Venezuela, daily El Nacional, for example, reported on October 14, 1982, that "while scores of torturers and drug-runners are fleeing the extensive evidence left behind is providing lists of names, financial country channels, and safehouses to the investigators in the government of the new president." According to the report, "the 'cocaine group' crowd around ousted dictator Garcia Meza was run by Argentine operatives of the Italy-centered Propaganda-2 Freemasonic lodge."

Mexican officials were neither agitated nor threatened by the P-2 scandal, because their nation has been run by Grand Orient Freemasonry since 1928. The National Revolutionary Party (Partido Revolucionario Institucional, or PRI), has been the ruling party since Mexico won its 100-year-old Masonic revolution in 1928. The PRI is the official political party of Grand Orient Freemasonry in Mexico, and its politicians are all Grand Orient Masons. In fact, since the ouster of the Mafia from Cuba by Castro in 1960, Masonic lodges in Mexico have worked hand in glove with terrorist Cuban exile organizations in Florida to assist in Mexican drug trafficking in that state. For example, a few months before the P-2 scandal broke in the summer of 1982, Mexican Carlos Vazquez Rangel, a 33rd degree Grand Orient Freemason, traveled to the anti-Castro secret centers in Florida and New York to enlist the participation of their Masonic branches in his Mexican drug trafficking effort. Rangel at that time was trying to work his way into the Grand Orient-controlled

PRI government of the newly elected president, Miguel de la Madrid through his fellow Mason, Mayor of Mexico City, Carlos Hank Gonzalez. A few years earlier, Mayor Gonzalez had rapidly built and paid for out of his own funds a Masonic front organization called the National Confederation of Liberal Organizations, and had incorporated it into the PRI. Rangel was its director. The Confederation was believed to have been a front for the infamous Propaganda-2 dope-trafficking Masonic Lodge of Italy. At the October 12–15 Mexican Grand Masonic Convention of 1982, run by Vazquez Rangel, Mayor Gonzalez received the 33rd degree rank as a Mason, amidst much publicity. Vazquez Rangel admitted to investigate that he was close to the infamous Propaganda-2 Lodge of Italy's Licio Gelli, and knew of seventeen members of the P-2 Lodge in Mexico. He refused to reveal whether Hank Gonzalez's "Confederation" was part of P-2.

Throughout the latter half of 1982, P-2 Freemasonry was on the lips of every politician in every nation in Latin and South America, and in Europe and England. Only in America were we kept ignorant, primarily because Freemasonry controls our news media.

English Freemasonry's Revenge

Before the news broke of the Masonic ritual murder of Calvi in the of 1982, the British had already begun an investigation of Banco Ambrosiano, which had gone into receivership. By early 1982 they discovered that Calvi and his Vatican friends had stolen a total of billion from their banks in London and Switzerland. Yallop writes:

The $1.3 billion hole in Banco Ambrosiano was not only created by the fraudulent purchase of shares in Calvi's own bank. Many millions went to sustain Gelli... For example, Calvi diverted $65 million from Peru to a numbered account at UBS Zurich.

The owner of that account is Licio Gelli.

In early 1982 Calvi transferred direct from the mother bank in Milan $470 million to the bank in Peru. He then gave his secretary a plane ticket to Monte Carlo and a pile of telex messages. The messages, duly sent from Monte Carlo, moved the money into a variety of Swiss numbered accounts.

Although this information alone was enough for British Freemasonry to assassinate Calvi, it was not all he had done to them on Gelli's orders. Calvi was moving these huge sums of money in an effort to bring to completion Gelli's final plan to capture all of English Freemasonry's Central and South American drug business. In 1982, London began searching for Gelli.

The Falklands War

Licio Gelli was a man on the run. He first fled to Argentina until things cooled down. While there, he devised a plan for moving his center operation out of the "hotbed" of Rome and into the British-controlled Falkland Islands. The Falklands seemed to Gelli to be the perfect center for a new Hong Kong-style of banking. He determined that London had no stomach for war, nor any interest in the Falklands.

Gelli talked the Argentine junta into moving militarily against the islands, promising them financial assistance. At Gelli's instructions, Calvi furnished several millions to the military regime that controlled Argentina. Money stolen by Calvi from British banks and diverted to his Banco Ambrosiano in Peru was used by the Argentinean military junta to purchase Exocet missiles from the French, which were to be used against the British during the Falklands War.

> "It is not pleasant," writes Yallop, "to reflect that patriotic British citizens undoubtedly financed the purchase of Exocet missiles for Argentina, missiles that killed many British soldiers during the Falklands war."

After the Falklands War, English Freemasonry went after Robe Calvi. It is not known whether Calvi took it upon himself to go to

London, or if he was kidnapped and brought there. At any rate he traveled by way of Austria. Yallop says that "Calvi, at Gelli's suggestion, traveled to London and to his death."

Possibly Gelli set up Calvi as a scapegoat, hoping his death satisfy London. If so, it failed, for English Freemasonry went after as well, who at that time was hiding in South America. It would be simple task to capture Gelli. His secret bank accounts were in Switzerland. The British Masonic oligarchy controlled the Swiss banks. In August 1982, two months after Calvi's death, Gelli began encountering a problem with one his accounts in Geneva. It was not performing order. Every time he attempted to transfer money, the UBS in Geneva declined to comply with the instructions. Gelli was told that he would have to appear at the bank in person. Using a fake Argentinean passport Gelli flew to Madrid and then to Geneva on September 13, 1982. He presented his documentation at the bank and was told there would be a short delay. Minutes later, he was arrested. Extradition proceedings began immediately from Italy. For one year, the Italian government tried to extradite Gelli, but to no avail. On August 10, 1983, Gelli escaped from his prison cell in Geneva. The evidence points to outside help. Gelli had been drugged and carried away. By whom, we can only speculate.

Obviously, this kidnapping was not a P-2 operation to keep Gelli silent otherwise he would have been killed in prison. Subsequent evidence (explained later) reveals that he was kidnapped by English Freemasonry, and for a special reason. He was more important to London alive than dead.

Repercussions and Gelli's Surrender

The repercussions of the P-2 scandal unlocked the mystery of the so called "terrorist" activities that had plagued Europe since the mid-1970s, such as the 1980 bombing of the Bologna train station that killed eighty five people. On December 13, 1985, the New York Times reported that the fugitive, Licio Gelli, along with other P-2 members, was indicted for "masterminding" the attack.

The P-2 scandal almost toppled the Italian government, with prime Minister Bettino Craxi of Italy announcing his resignation on March 3 in Rome. Wearied by his four years of unrelenting investigations into the P-2 affair the resignation stepped down. Ironically, the party which assumed power Craxi's resignation was the Christian Democrats, the same party that battered by scandals, including the involvement of its senior party leaders in P-2.

Six months later on September 21, 1987, Licio Gelli surrendered to authorities at Geneva, Switzerland. The New York Times reported that "by, surrendering here, Mr. Gelli was assured that if he is returned to Italy under the existing Swiss court order he could only be tried on fraud, defamation and bankruptcy charges accepted by the Swiss court years ago." Why would Gelli surrender to authorities inside the stronghold of the British Freemasonic oligarchy? He had fought them in the Falklands. With the assistance of the late Roberto Calvi, he had stolen $1.3 billion from them. Why would he return to Switzerland and not to Italy where his ruling party was in power? For some reason, Gelli's life had been spared by the British. Gelli was a man of unusual charisma, capable of surrounding himself with the political leaders of the world; he was a man capable of bringing down the Italian government; he was a man who had engineered the theft of $1.3 billion from British banks. Such a man must not be wasted, but exploited.

Gelli alone could unravel the web he had woven in South America. During the four years between his kidnapping from the Geneva prison cell and his surrender to Swiss authorities, English Masonic operatives were with Gelli visiting P-2 lodges throughout Central and South America unraveling the web he had spun about British Freemasonry.

Today, English Freemasonry completely controls the P-2 operation throughout Central and South America, including Mexico. In December 1994, the American news media reported that the heads of the South American drug cartels and the British-controlled drug lords of the Golden Triangle in the Orient, gathered in Geneva to discuss combining their world-wide drug operations. Their purpose for uniting could only be to escalate London's drug war against the United States of America, to ensure its final destruction. Only by destroying the U.S.A. can the whore of Babylon rule the world.

Chapter 7

LONDON'S DRUG WAR AGAINST AMERICA

Spiritism is the fundamental mystery of most secret societies and the drug traffic is its chief commercial.

Edith Starr Miller - 1933

Drugs have long been a powerful weapon in the hands of the conspirators. That is why drugs cannot be eliminated.

Dr. John Coleman 1985

The primary purpose for English Freemasonry's global network of drug traffickers was and is to fuel Great Britain's economy. In the early years of the empire, Great Britain had no industry but trade cotton in exchange for silk, spices, and opium from the Orient, and the trade in African slaves. The banking industry necessarily developed from her trade, and expanded worldwide following the Second Opium War. London's second purpose for maintaining a global network of drug traffickers was and is to declare a drug war against the United States of America, partly in revenge for losing America to our revolutionary war, and partly for stripping our assets. To accomplish this task, three Masonic frameworks were set up by the end of the Second Opium War. At the head of each framework were the following 33rd degree Freemasons: Henry Palmerston in England, Albert Pike in America, and Giuseppe Mazzini in Italy.

In 1855, 33rd degree Freemason Henry Palmerston was elected Prime Minister of Great Britain.

A Masonic prime minister was essential for maintaining communications with heads of state, so he could be keep abreast of any anti-drug activity within the nations of operation. Palmerston also stayed in touch with Pike and Mazzini to inform them of orders he had issued to London's drug network in the Orient. Nearly every inhabitant of England's political, financial and mercantile netherworld, including the Masonic drug lords of the British East India Company, followed a chain of command that led back through English Freemasonry directly to Lord Palmerston and his successors.

In 1859, Albert Pike was elected Grand Commander of the supreme Council of the Southern Jurisdiction of Freemasonry at Charleston S.C. From his powerful position, Pike engineered the secession of the southern states from the Union, and then opened the doors of America to foreign drug traffickers.

In 1860, Giuseppe Mazzini ended his futile attempt to unite Italy under republicanism. His gang of Masonic hoodlums were in desperate need of a lucrative source of income. Trafficking heroin from the Orient to the United States afforded them that income.

Before his death in 1865, Lord Palmerston, Albert Pike, and Giuseppe Mazzini were destined to unite the hierarchy of Freemasonry against Christian America. It would take less than a century before the effects of their scheme to destroy our nation with drug addiction could be realized.

To Freemasons, however, time is not an enemy, but an ally. In the conspiracy of Freemasonry, the soldier dies, but the war continues.

English Freemasonry and the Mafia

By the mid-1830s, Mazzini had organized and commanded a group of Masonic Lodges for youth called "Young Italy." These lodges spread rapidly throughout Europe and Great Britain. In England, the Prime Minister who followed Palmerston was Freemason Benjamin Disraeli (1804–1881); he launched the "Young Englanders." In Russia. Freemason Alexander Herzen initiated Freemason Mikhail Bakunin (1814–1876) into a similar bomb-throwing society. In the United States of America it was the pre-Civil War terrorist, John Brown, who led Young America on a murderous rampage. All in all, Young Societies were organized in Italy, England, America, Switzerland, Germany, Poland, Russia, Turkey, and Serbia. Young Serbia, the Masonic Lodge that plotted and carried out the assassination of Archduke Ferdinand which triggered World War I, was destined to join hands with Young Italy in the drug war against America.

In short, members of the Young Societies were hoodlums trained to do the bidding of Universal Freemasonry. Their main objective the help was of this spread Masonic revolution throughout Europe. With rabble from Young Italy, Mazzini brought his Masonic revolution to Italy. Having no skills or aims other than raising havoc, these Italian thugs supported themselves by robbing banks, kidnapping for ransom, and looting or burning businesses if their proprietors refused to pay for protection. With Mazzini as their leader, the word spread that "Mazzini autorizza furti, incendi, e attentati." (translated: "Mazzini authorizes Theft, arson, and Kidnapping.") Shortened to the acronym "M.A.F.I.A.", organized crime was born.

The Mafia afforded London an experienced international don bureau capable of eliminating any head of state who hindered English Freemasonry's narcotics objectives. In the same way that the Chinese Triads took orders from English Freemasonry and money from the narcotics trade in the East, the Mafia did likewise in West.

The Mafia: A British Protectorate

English Freemasonry has been, and is to this day, the protector of the Mafia. This fact was confirmed in 1982, the year the predominantly Mafia-run Propaganda Duo Masonic Lodge scandal broke at Rome. That year the Italian government revealed that the P-2 Lodge was responsible for the 1978 assassinations of both Italian Prime Minister Aldo Moro and Pope John Paul I. The first Pope John Paul was murdered after he discovered that English Masonic bankers were cooperating with P-2 Lodge operatives within the Vatican to launder Mafia drug money through the Vatican Bank.

The Italian government's 1982 investigation into the P-2 scandal was precipitated by the attempted assassination of the second Pope John Paul, who survived the attempt by a "lone gunman" on May 13, 1981. When Freemasonry was implicated, France, dominated by Grand Orient Freemasonry, tried to shift blame to communist Bulgaria. The leading Paris daily, Le Monde—which publishes reports favorable to the Craft—claimed on December 3, 1982, that

> "Soviet factional opponents of former KGB head Yuri Andropov were suspected to be behind revelations of a Bulgarian connection to the May 13, 1981 attempt to assassinate Pope John Paul II."

P-2 Freemasonry and the Plot to Kill the Pope

Based upon subsequent evidence, the Le Monde article was a classic example of Masonic disinformation. The Bulgarian government launched its own investigation for the purpose of clearing its name and discovered that the controllers of Mehmet Ali Agca, the would-be assassin of the pope, were Turkish Mafia figure Bekir Celenk and two Italian spies being held in Bulgaria.

In direct response to the international spotlight on the Celenk case, the Bulgarian government announced on December 22,

1982, that it was placing the two accused Italian spies, Paolo Farsetti and his girlfriend Gabriella Trevisini, on trial. The charge, according to the Bulgarian report, was that the pair were agents of a Masonic called Propaganda 2 (P-2), which gave the order to assassinate the pope.

Pope John Paul was well aware that the attempt made on his life was by the same Mafia figures within the P-2 Lodge who had assassinated his predecessor. In the fall of 1982, the Vicar of Christ therefore called for the Italian government to wage war against the Mafia. The Carabinieri, Italy's anti-terrorist national police, swung into action. Its investigation revealed that the Mafia had been backed and protected by the British since its founding in the middle of the nineteenth century. Unfortunately this information surfaced upon the September 3, 1982, assassination in Sicily of Carabinieri General Carlo Dalla Chiesa—three months after he had been sent there with extraordinary powers to wage war against the Mafia. The general's bereaved assistant gave an anonymous interview to the Catholic newspaper, Sabato, in which he said: By studying the history of Sicily, both Dalla Chiesa and I reached the same conclusions. In 1796 the Bourbons of Naples escaped to Sicily where they lived protected by the British Navy until after the Battle of Waterloo. From that time on, the island became a British protectorate... It was with the support of England that in 1860 (33rd degree Freemason General) Garibaldi landed in Sicily... In 1874, when England decided it was necessary to bring to power the revolutionary left, which was more monarchist than the king, it gave money and financial backing to the very powerful Masonic and Anglophile Florio family to help [Freemason and Mafia figure] Crispi and his gang. In the elections of 1874, with the help of the Mafia, the left won 48 out of 48 seats in Sicily...

This interview of the assistant to the late General Dalla Chiesa presented historical data that the Mafia had been sustained by both the British navy and Freemasonry for over a century. Likewise, both the Italian and Bulgarian governments' investigations concluded that British Masonic bankers, the Mafia, and the P-2 Masonic Lodge cooperated in laundering Mafia drug money through the Vatican Bank. This money trail was evidence of the network London had established following the Second Opium War. America was the target for London's next drug war.

The 100-Year Plan to Destroy America with Drugs

It took the British a century (from 1729 to 1830) to sap the wealth of Imperial China by drug addiction. London calculated that it would take At least as long to decimate the economy of the United States. English Freemasonry began her drug war against America shortly after the First Chinese Opium War (1840–1842), when her "merchants of the sea" began selling Chinese indentured slaves (called the "coolie trade") on the west coast of America, using them as the initial conduit for drugs into our nation. The authors of Dope, Inc. (1978) explain: In 1846 alone, 117,000 coolies were brought into the country, feeding an opium trade estimated at nearly 230,000 pounds of gum opium and over 53,000 pounds of prepared (smoking) opium. Although Lincoln outlawed the coolie trade in 1862, the black marketeering in Chinese … continued at an escalating rate through to the end of the century.

While the coolie trade continued in America, the Italian revolutionaries under Mazzini's command appeared to be stonewalled in their twenty-five year effort to bring republicanism to Italy. In 1860, with England's navy returning home from its Second Opium War, Mazzini petitioned Prime Minister Lord Palmerston for financial and naval assistance. Soon afterwards Mazzini made a push to unite Italy, while General Garibaldi conquered Sicily with assistance from the British Navy.

Palmerston's cooperation with Mazzini had broader implications. Mazzini's Mafia (already proven to be identical in political character to the ruthless Oriental Triads) would open the West to drugs in the same manner as the Triads had opened the East. With the Mafia in control of Sicily, London used the island nation as a hub for heroin distribution in the West.

Albert Pike's Civil War

Albert Pike's part in the grand scheme of British Freemasonry's war against America had two phases. First, he was to divide America by civil war by guaranteeing that the southern states would secede from the Union. Second, he was to open the doors of the South to the Mafia. Once Pike completed his tasks, London would use the Mafia to initiate the drug war against America.

In 1859, Albert Pike, the grand philosopher of Freemasonry, gained control of the Southern Jurisdiction of Freemasonry. With his Masonic surrogates positioned throughout the South, Pike called for a state-by-state secession from the Union. Prior to and during the American Civil War, London began to initiate her drug war against unsuspecting America. The authors of *Dope, Inc.* (1978), elaborate:

> British pharmaceutical houses had begun commercial and production made large of morphine quantities in the years to leading both armies. The British firms misrepresented the morphine as "nonaddictive" pain killer and even had the audacity to push it as a cure rot opium addiction.

After the Civil War, drug-addicted veterans now to be supplied with opium. The confusion caused by post-war Reconstruction in the South created the distractions necessary for Albert Pike to open door Mafia drug suppliers. When Mazzini sent his lieutenants into the United States, the veterans of Young Italy moved into channel, already carved out by Albert Pike; thus was the second phase of Pike's, grand scheme completed. At this point, English Freemasonry adopted two strategies to spread drug use and addiction throughout America. First, the Mafia would work from the bottom up, using the "underworld" element of society to establish distribution networks. Second, the educated class would work from the top down, using college professors and other members of the elite to influence and alter the thinking and attitudes of their students by suggesting they experiment with drugs. The first project would be rapid and ruthless. The second would take less than a century.

From the Bottom Up: Ethnic Mafias

The first recorded evidence of organized crime activity in America identifies the Mazzini networks with General Pike's KKK guerrilla war against the forces of "Reconstruction" in the South. Both before and/during the Civil War, the Mafia's "port of entry" was New Orleans. The first-known Mafia leader in the United States was a Mason named Joseph Macheca, who organized and commanded a company of Sicilians in the early 1860s. After Albert Pike founded the Ku Klux Klan in 1867, the activities of the Macheca gang were indistinguishable from those of the Klan. Another who fled Sicily in the early 1870s, arriving in New Orleans to make contact with Macheca, was a close associate of Mazzini, Freemason Giuseppe Esposito. Esposito traveled throughout the United States, uniting the various lodges of Italian Freemasonry and establishing inter city communications between them where none had existed before these ethnic Masonic lodges gave birth to our organized crime syndicates in America.

The implantation of ethnic Freemasonry into America by the turn of the twentieth century is too complex a story to cover in this book. These ethnic networks, however, became so intertwined that, for general purposes, the name "organized crime" applies to them all. Three, however, are especially significant and worthy of mention. The first is the Jewish Bronfman Family that emigrated to Canada and built their fortunes on distilling "spirits" during prohibition days. Today they own Seagram's. The male members of this family were, and are, members of Jewish Freemasonry, transferred funds from English Freemasonry for the assassination of President John F. Kennedy.

The second group is the Chinese Coolies who were "shanghaied" to the West Coast, and who smuggled dope into the country through their Masonic-style Triads. The Triads continue to operate in our nation today, mainly in Chinatowns. In recent years, however, they have mysteriously branched out into large cities, setting up networks of organized crime from coast to coast.

Just as mysterious are the Chinese boat-people who attempted to land on American shores in the spring and summer of 1993. Our government estimates that 1.5 million Chinese annually are smuggled from mainland China into the United States by these and other means. It is too early to tell, but based upon past history, some of these Chinese "immigrants" may be coming to America to help the Triads handle the increased drug traffic that is expected upon the opening of our northern and southern borders with the passage of the North America Free Trade Agreement—NAFTA. (NAFTA was signed into law in San Antonio, Texas on October 7, 1993.

Since then, according to statistics reported in December 1994, drug use has doubled in the U.S.) It is interesting to recall that the British fought the Chinese Opium Wars to enforce "free trade," so that goods traded across borders in China (specifically opium from India) would not be inspected.

The third group of note is the Masonic Serbo-Croatian "Black Hand" gangs that entered America through New York in the 1890s. In 1901, Freemason Con Vito Cascioferro arrived in New York from Palermo to help form ties between the Black Hand and the Sicilian Mafia. Controlling this hodge-podge of ethnic Masonic lodges was the overarching Sicilian Mafia—English Freemasonry's hired gun.

From the Top Down: The Intelligentsia

London's second drug war offensive against America was planned from the top down, employing the intelligentsia. Although delayed until after World War I, the plan to penetrate America's upper-class society by means of the intelligentsia began during the Opium Wars. At that time many Masonic researchers were investigating eastern religions in order to discover the origins of Freemasonry. As they read each other's research, they realized how much of their work was repetitious. In the 1870s Freemason Sir Walter Desant, brother of Theosophist Annie Besant, suggested to Freemason W.R.

Rylands, author of Masons' Works, that they should form a research lodge that would catalog all data in order to eliminate duplication in their work. Acting upon Besant's suggestion, Rylands started a movement to form such a lodge. In 1884 a petition to form a research lodge had been signed by nine Prominent British Masons and presented to the Grand Master of the Grand Lodge of England, Albert Edward, Prince of Wales (who later became Ring Edward VII). On November 28, Prince Edward signed the warrant granting certification to a research lodge. Two years later, on January 12, 1886, the Quatuor Coronati Lodge of Masonic Research, n° 2076, opened its doors in London. Its first meeting was attended on April 7, 1886, by six of the original nine petitioners, who adopted by-laws limiting its membership to forty.

The six original members of the Quatuor Coronati Lodge included (1) London's Chief of Police, Commissioner Sir Charles Warren of Jack the Ripper cover-up fame (Warren was elected first Worshipful Master); (2) Barrister Robert Freke Gould, author of Gould's History of Freemasonry, a book that traces the religious philosophy of Freemasonry back to Babylon; (3) Anglican Rector, Rev. Adolphus Frederick Alexander Woodford, a prolific writer who authored Defense of Masonry in an attempt to prove that Freemasonry is compatible with Christianity, (4) Archaeologist William James Hughan; (5) George William Speth, the originator, a year later, of the Correspondence Circle of the Quatuor Coronati Lodge; and (6) Shadwell H. Clerke, Grand Secretary of the lodge. In his Encyclopedia of Freemasonry, Dr. Mackey announces in orphic language that the assignment of the Quatuor Coronati was (as it is today) to study pagan religions throughout the world to find the roots of Freemasonry: This Lodge, n° 2076 on the Roll of the Grand Lodge Of England, was established in 1886, for the purpose of studying the History, Symbols, and Legends of Freemasonry, and it is in fact a Masonic Literary and Archaeological Society, meeting as a titled Lodge. Attached to the Lodge proper, which is limited to forty full members, is a Correspondence Circle established in 1887, and later numbering several thousand members drawn from all parts of the world... All Master Masons in good standing are eligible to membership in the Correspondence Circle.

Ars Quatuor Coronatorum are the volumes of transactions published each year since its constitution in 1886 by the Quatuor Coronati Lodge of Research… With their more than fifty volumes the Ars are now a larger set of books than the Encyclopaedia Britannica, and perform the function for Masonic knowledge that is performed by the Britannica and similar works for general knowledge; since almost every contributor to the Ars has been a trained scholar, (or) at least has been a specialist in some field of scholarship, the academic standards are higher than those of popular encyclopedias.

Quatuor Coronati Lodge of Research … has long since become the supreme court of learning and authority in Masonic scholarship throughout the world… It has carried out more successfully the command, 'Let there be light' than any other single agency thus far manned by Craftsmen…

In The Great Teachings of Masonry, 33rd degree Freemason H.L. Haywood confirms that the research conducted by the Quatuor Coronati is for Masonic use: An institution which demands so high an educational ideal on the part of the outside world should … set a shining example. This is the whole pith and contention of … the Quatuor Coronati Lodge in London … to further the cause of Masonic education… Masonic Research does not mean a delving into the dust bins of antiquity for rare lore—it means a digging out of Masonry that which there is now in it for truth, and for light.

Haywood goes on to confirm that the other purpose of the Quatuor Coronati is to apply its discoveries to present-day Masonic work the result of which has brought a century of paganism to Europe and the United States, rivaling the paganism of antediluvian days.

Fruit of the Quatuor Coronati

Based upon subsequent events which immediately followed the opening of the Quatuor Coronati Lodge, we know that the research lodge made three important discoveries about ancient mystery religions: (1) all pagan gods and goddesses represent the hermaphroditic Lucifer; (2) the Babylonian priesthood used drugs and sex as a means of controlling people; and (3) human sacrifice was employed as a means of limiting population growth.

To apply these three discoveries to present-day Masonic Quatuor Coronati Lodge established several sub-lodges of a degenerate nature to disseminate its new findings throughout British society. These sub-lodges (sometimes called co-Masonry, because women are to join) did not retain or use the name "Masonry" in their creation. Nonetheless, all these organizations were founded by 33rd degree Masons. To save face by disassociation, the Grand Lodge of England did not recognize these particular bodies of Masonry. Co-Masonic groups, however, have always recognized and admitted Masons of all regularly constituted Masonic orders, both English and French.

With the creation of these sub-Masonic lodges, witchcraft and drug use began to spread everywhere, even into the highest circles of British life. Satanic jewelry became commonplace.

Rituals that incorporated mind-altering drugs, orgies, and human sacrifice were discreetly out in the heart of the London slums and on remote ancestral estates.

The first of these Masonic sub-lodges was the Hermetic Order of Golden Dawn, founded in 1887 by three Rosicrucian Masons. Ver A.F.A. Woodford (1821–1887), one of the original founders of the Quatuor Coronati Lodge, provided Dr. William Wynn Westcott (1848–1923), a well-know cabalist, with documentation from the Correspondence Circle that would form the basis for the drug-using and sex-codifying Golden Dawn. Also assisting in the founding of the Golden Dawn was 32nd degree Freemason Sam Liddell MacGregor Mathers, another well-know cabalist.

These three Masons were soon joined by three more Masons: Spiritualist and poet William Butler Yeats (1865–1939); Satanist Aleister Crowley (1875–1947), the man who was to become known worldwide his practice of black magic; and Luciferian Helena Blavatsky (1831–1891), a female Mason who remained a member of the Golden Dawn until her death.

Cross-Connections

Twelve years earlier, in 1875, Madam Blavatsky had founded the Theosophical Society in New York City. One of her first initiates was Albert Pike. To have immediate access to the newly-formed Correspondence Circle of the Quatuor Coronati Lodge, Blavatsky moved to London in 1887 where she started her Theosophical magazine, Lucifer the Light-Bringer, and published Secret Doctrine and Isis Unveiled. She gleaned most of her documentation for these works from the Circle of the Research Lodge.

In 1889, Annie Besant, upon introduction to Madame Blavatsky succumbed to her irresistible magnetism and formidable power of gestion and joined the Theosophical Society. That same year, MacGregor Mathers wrote a letter to Blavatsky in which he stated that the Theosophical Society and the Golden Dawn had much in common, and he invited Blavatsky to join the Golden Dawn.

After Blavatsky's death in 1891, the founding members of the Quatuor Coronati Lodge lobbied for Sir Walter Desant's sister, Annie Besant, to be made president of the Theosophical Society; Annie Besant (1847–1933), a brilliant speaker and a member or the Fabian Society, a socialist network of Freemasons, finally became president of the Theosophical Society in 1904. Annie immediately turned the Theosophical Society into a recruitment center not only for the Golden Dawn, but also for Aleister Crowley's homicidal sub-lodge Ordo Templi Orientis (O.T.O.).

The Order of the Golden Dawn in turn created two homicidal sub-lodges of its own, the Order of the Temple of the East (in 1895) and the Thule Society (in 1917). The Temple of the East was later absorbed by Aleister Crowley's Ordo Templi Orientis. Both the Thule and the Temple of the East were breeding grounds for the inner core of the Hitler movement.

George Orwell's Exposé

In the 1920s Aleister Crowley inducted Freemason George Orwell (1903–1950) into the drug cult lodge of the Golden Dawn. Orwell was so overcome with the evil planned for America by this diabolical new age order that he felt compelled to write a novel as a warning to America. Two years before he died he finished this work, entitled 1984. The year of the title had nothing to do with a prophetic timetable, but was picked by Orwell by reversing 1948, the year of the book's completion.

Like so many "insiders" (i.e., those who are privy to information about and the machinations of the conspirators), Orwell could not keep this devilish secret, nor could he directly expose it upon penalty of death. Therefore, Orwell published his novel after the death of Aleister Crowley in 1947 in order to shed light in an indirect manner on the course of events through which English Freemasonry planned to take control of the United States of America during the latter half of the twentieth century.

In 1984, the chief conspirator asks a young man who desires to join the "Big Brother" (Masonic) fraternity the following question:

Are you prepared to give your life? To commit murder? To commit acts of sabotage which may cause the death of hundreds of innocent people? To betray your country to foreign powers? To cheat, to forge, to blackmail, to corrupt the minds of children, to distribute habit-forming drugs, to encourage prostitution to disseminate venereal diseases; to do anything which is likely to cause demoralization and weaken the power of the people? Are you prepared to commit suicide, if and when we order you to do so?

Far from being a prophecy of a communist takeover of America, many supposed it to be, *1984* was a novelistic exposé of how Mason in conspirators planned to weaken the United States by creating a population who would be incapable of resistance. This British design for America is a blueprint now in its final phase of execution under the Anglophile Clinton administration; this plan is being perpetrated and promoted by English Freemasonry and its subversive supporters, Rhodes Scholars.

The Elite and Drugs in America

At approximately the same time that Aleister Crowley inducted George Orwell into the Golden Dawn, English Freemasonry, through its Royal Institute of International Affairs (RIIA) and its psychological warfare arm, the Tavistock Institute, was preparing other intellectuals to send to America. Aldous Huxley (1894–1963) and his brother Julian (1887–1975), grandsons of Freemason T.H. Huxley (1825–1895), had both been under the Masonic tutelage of 33rd degree Freemason H.G. Wells (1866 1946). In the 1920s, Wells directed the brothers to Aleister Crowley for further training. Crowley inducted them into the Golden Dawn drug using cult where they were trained on how to subvert a nation through drug addiction. In the 1930s, Aldous Huxley, by then a well-known writer, was deployed by the RIIA to Hollywood to mentor and influence those who would create what was known in the 1960s as the rock-drug sex counterculture—and what today has permeated our whole culture. Aldous Huxley, although not a college professor, used his writings influence the college intelligentsia throughout the 1950s and 1960s who in turn would influence their students.

The LSD cult was the creation of the Royal Institute of International Affairs. On the RIIA membership rolls were some of the elite psychiatrists of Europe. Beginning in the late 1940s and continuing through the 1950s, the use of drugs in the educated circles of Europe began with these psychiatrists, who experimented with LSD in training sessions to better understand their psychotic patients and the nature of psychosis. Aldous Huxley made this drug available to U.S.

Naval Intelligence to assist in designing the first LSD experiments in techniques for mass subversion of youth populations. In 1947 the CIA joined the project under the code name "MK-U1tra"; the CIA spent $26 million tax dollars over the next twenty-five years for covert experiments with the behavior of the American public." Using guidelines much like those described in George Orwell's novel 1984, the CIA wanted to see, at home, if it was possible to erase memories and create apathy.

Director of the CIA during most of this period was the Anglophile Allen Dulles (1893–1969), who with his brother John, was a founding member of English Freemasonry's Council on Foreign Relations (CFR). Allen Dulles was trained in spying and counter-espionage in 1941 under freemason and O.T.O. spokesman William (Wild Bill) Donovan, who was founder of the Office of Strategic Services (OSS), forerunner of the CIA. From October 1942 to May 1945, Dulles served as chief of the OSS office in Bern, Switzerland, where he assisted in screening captive Nazi SS officers for future use by American and British intelligence. In 1951, Dulles was appointed deputy director of the CIA under Gen. Walter Bedell Smith. In 1953, during the tenure of his brother John as secretary of state, Allen was appointed director of the CIA by President Eisenhower. In 1961, when John F. Kennedy moved into the White House, he reappointed Dulles as CIA director, but put a stop to the LSD experiment. Two years after Kennedy's assassination, the CIA launched its MK-Ultra project again, this time on an expanded scale, with the distribution of 100 million doses of LSD-25 on U.S. campuses.

In the beginning years of the MK-Ultra project, Aldous Huxley wrote a book entitled The Doors of Perception (1954), which had a twofold purpose: (1) it sent a message to his British Masonic masters that his LSD project was underway; and (2) it drew many more to experiment not only with LSD, but with other drugs as well. Among his most devoted followers were college professors and their students, who had read his writings religiously. Huxley lauded the effects of experimentation with mescaline as beneficial for most, with only a minority suffering ill-effects: "Along with the happily transfigured majority of mescaline takers there is a minority that finds in the drug only hell and purgatory."

Non-medical interest in LSD and related drugs began to grow during the 1950s, primarily among experimenters in the academic, professional, and artistic fields. LSD in particular gained more notoriety in the early 1960s as a result of experimentation by two Harvard psychology professors, Dr. Richard Alpert and Timothy Leary, who invited others to "turn on, tune in, and drop out" of the existing social institutions. Their unorthodox religious approach to the LSD experience is presented in a manual Called The Psychedelic Experience, which is based on the Tibetan Book Of the Dead. This manual became the bible of the psychedelic drug movement.

In 1966, Leary started his own religion, the League of Spiritual Discovery, using LSD as its sacrament. Richard Alpert, who had studied under the guidance of a guru in India, left LSD behind and graduated to the "high" of meditation. He is now called Baba Ram Dass and has a following in the United States. He lectures to many groups and directs meditative retreats.

The Masonic Counterculture

Many people in America today now realize the disaster that has been wrought upon our culture since the "counterculture" revolution of the 1960s. But few understand or know how this culture war was prepared for by English Freemasonry, which launched her drug war against America through her Masonic rock groups. According to Mackey's Encyclopedia of Freemasonry, there are in England today Masonic lodges for musicians—identical to those on the Continent frequented by Mozart and others—where artists meet to discuss their mutual objectives to spread Masonic revolution through song.

Edith Miller in Occult Theocrasy (1933) explains that music is an essential tool of the Masonic conspiracy, because it renders an otherwise positive mind passive and negative. Miller states that occult music tends to induce confusion. Minds that are confused will obey and bow to the influences of the hidden masters and eventually become negative toward family, country, and God. We shall see the result of this negative lifestyle in the course of our study. A person who does not listen to this music, and replaces it with uplifting activity, remains positive. A positive mind cannot be controlled.

In Death Cults (1984), Dr. John Coleman, a former British intelligence agent, also details how English Freemasonry is behind the rock-drug-sex counterculture. He says that "rock music is a vehicle for the distribution of drugs, and a means of controlling the minds of the Young. This is directly linked to death cults through English Freemason Aldous Huxley's experiments on the west coast of the USA. Huxley's followers dished out LSD to rock groups for distribution at their concerts."

The Beatles were the first British rock group to be deployed to the United States by the drug barons of London. Although it is easy to connect English Freemasonry to many British rock and roll stars, it is difficult to connect the Beatles directly to the London lodges. The Beatles did, however, have a fascination for Masons and things Masonic. For example, on the front cover of The Beatles' album Sgt. Pepper is appears to be a group portrait. Some of the figures are known freemasons of yesteryear, including Aleister Crowley, a 33rd degree Grand orient Mason and Grand Master of three degenerate British Masonic orders; Karl Marx, a 32nd degree Grand Orient Mason, who spent his latter years in England; Carl Jung, a Rosicrucian Freemason; and H.G. Wells, a 33rd degree English Mason. When Ringo Starr was asked in an interview why they picked these people, he said, "We just thought we would like to put together a lot of people we like and admire."

Freemason and Satanist Aleister Crowley was their favorite. And like Crowley, Beatle John Lennon was deeply involved in the occult. Numerology and the Tarot were favorites of both.

Moreover, much of what Crowley believed and taught was based on tantric Hinduism. All the Beatles at one time or another experimented with aspects of this eastern religious philosophy.

Beatle George Harrison, for example, wholeheartedly accepted and adopted Hinduism as his own, and his songs reflect that fact: "Within You Without You" on the Sgt. Pepper album; "Life Itself" on his solo album Somewhere in England; and "My Sweet Lord" from his three-record-set tribute to Hinduism called All things Must Pass. In an interview with the Rolling Stone magazine in 1987, Harrison admitted that his past excursion into devil worship in the temple of Kali (the Hindu goddess of death) in Calcutta, India, was instigated by the powerful drug, LSD. He said in the magazine interview, "When I was younger with the effects of the LSD that opened something up inside me in 1966, a flood of other thoughts came into my head, which led me to the yogis."

The authors of Dope, Inc. (1986) confirm that the British "deployment of the Beatles into the United States [overlaps] both the distribution of LSD-25 dosages and the penetration of the burgeoning 'New Left' with the rock-drug-sex counterculture, which set the counterculture into motion to become a mass movement by the late 1960s." Author Brian Key, who has studied the role of the media in the decline of our culture, has commented in his book, Media Sexploitation, that "The Beatles popularized the and culturally legitimatized hallucinatory drug usage among teenagers throughout the world... The Beatles became the super drug culture prophets and pushers of all times."

Names of the Beatles' songs witness their deep involvement in the drug Culture. For instance, "Day Tripper" can mean to take a shot of heroin in the morning and stay high all day; A "Yellow Submarine" in drug parlance is a yellow qualude, or downer; "Strawberxy Fields Forever" refers to poppy fields—poppy, the main ingredient of heroin, is red like and in "Hey Jude," jude can refer to marijuana."

Masonic Rock Stars

Mark Spaulding, a former drummer for a rock band, also connects English Freemasonry with the modern outbreak of anti-Christian rock and roll. In his book, The Heartbeat of the Dragon: The Occult Roots of Rock & Roll (1992), Spaulding traces the origins of modern rock and roll to the occult and drug lodges of English Freemasonry, and to other spiritualist groups: Through the late 1800's ... many British based, occult organizations were formed.

The Theosophical Society, The Hermetic Order of The Golden Dawn, The Order of The Silver Star, Freemasonry, and Rosicrucianism were but a few of the many esoteric that found their homes in England... The early 1960's England suddenly filled with people who were caught up in the occult; and British Rock & Roll was about to follow suit.

As the music of Freemason Mozart was used by the Brotherhood help initiate rebellion against the existing order prior to the French Revolution, Spaulding says that rock and roll was "specifically to instigate REBELLION in the listener ... as well as undermining their inborn God-ordained moral code."

Spaulding undertook extensive research on the occult origins and Satanic design of rock and roll.

His study led him to a sobering conclusion: "I have discovered evidence which clearly exposes an incredible interconnectedness between Rock & Roll, Hinduism, Shamanism, Satanism, and Voodoo... On the surface, these ideologies may seem to be quite diverse but deep within their core they are unmistakably identical."

This rise of Satanic rock music, drugs, shock-horror movies, and ritual Satanic murders is directly linked to English Masonry through its Hermetic Order of the Golden Dawn and the Ordo Templi Orientis (O.T.O.), both founded by 33rd degree Freemasons. By the time World War I had started, Crowley, a member of both English and French Freemasonry, was at the head of the British branch of both orders. Crowley encouraged his O.T.O. initiates to perform human sacrifices, using young boys as victims, while he himself is alleged to have taken part in 150 ritual murders.

The Ordo Templi Orientis was English Freemasonry's most effective psychological warfare unit.

Its duty was to attack and destroy Christian culture wherever it existed with an onslaught of Satanism. Maury Terry an American investigative journalist, in The Ultimate Evil, relates the story of how the O.T.O. got started in our country:

After internal dissension, elements of the Golden Dawn more or less merged into the Ordo Templi Orientis. Aleister Crowley won permission to head a British OTO branch, and the teachings of the OTO entered the United States with Crowley in 1916, during World War I in Europe.

After World War 1, Crowley helped establish an OTO lodge in Pasadena, California, and OTO branches subsequently sprouted in a number of U.S. cities, including New York and Houston. In effect, a loose network was formed and already functioning via occult shops and bookstores, newsletters, ads in the underground press and other methods...

In fact, many believe that the entire occult underground in America today can be traced back to the formation of that Crowley OTO operation in Pasadena.

Unfortunately, the O.T.O. did not go into decline after Aleister Crowley's death in 1947. Maury Terry has discovered its network thriving stronger than ever in America, and connects it to the recent surge of Satanic ritual murders. Included in this network are drug counterculture operatives, motorcycle gangs, common criminals and rock groups.

The fascination that rock stars have for English Freemasons, especially Aleister Crowley, and for things Masonic, at the least suggests the influence of English Freemasonry, and perhaps even stronger, direct ties. The following examples are drawn from the album jackets and lyrics of their songs:

1.

Britisher Lord David Sutch, or Screaming Lord Sutch, as he was affectionately called by his band, the Savages, had a passion for shocking horror show theatrics. For example, in one concert he entered stage in a black coffin borne by hooded monks. He emerged from the coffin with three spine chilling screams— headless and bloody with grotesque hands. A photograph of this was used for his album entitled Hands of Jack the Ripper. In chapter twenty of Scarlet and the Beast, volume one, we learned that the Ripper slayings were actually Masonic ritual murders.

2.

Ozzy Osbourne said that English Freemason Crowley was "the phenomenon of his time." Osbourne wrote a song about this Satanist entitled, "Mr. Crowley."

3.

Sting spent many hours reading Crowley's and Jung's occult books.

4.

Jim Morrison posed with a bust of Crowley for a band promo picture, which was used on the back of the Doors 13 album cover.

5.

Graham nond claimed to be Crowley's son. When he formed his "Holy Magick" band dedicated to Crowley, he spelled "Magick" in the Crowley fashion.

6.

The lyrics of Led Zeppelin's gong "Stairway to Heave" ,, include words used in the initiation ceremony of the Masonic Order of the Golden Dawn, an English Masonic order headed by Crowley.

7.

In an early W.A.S.P. stage show, Blackie Lawless drank blood from a human skull; this act is part of the initiation ceremony in the 30th degree of Scottish Rite Freemasonry.

8.

In the Rush album Hemispheres, Geddy Lee sings about the "brotherhood" doctrine of Freemasonry. In Rush's Witch Hunt, lyricist Neil Peart used the Masonic terms "Ignorance and prejudice" to refer to Christianity.

9.

In Venom's At War With Satan album, the lyrics define and praise the Masonic Russian Revolution of 1917: Damnation has sunk it's talons deep into the womb of utopia spilling forth great streams [of blood) of virginal purity and bliss. The golden throne of tetragrammaton [red star] is ablaze. His majesty (Satan) sits proud, the joyous drones of celebrations enact scenes of blasphemy, lust and destruction raping the Holy Trinity.

10.

Paul Kantner of Jefferson Airplane wrote lyrics like "Jesus had a son by Mary Magdalene." As we know, this doctrine comes straight from the lore of the Priory of Sion, the founding order of English Freemasonry.

11.

Jimi Hendrix also sings of the Priory of Sion legend:

The story of Jesus
so easy to explain
after they crucified him,
a woman, she (Mary Magdalene) claimed his name
The story of Jesus
the whole Bible knows
went all across the Desert
and in the middle, he found a rose (Rosicrucians)
There should be no questions
there should be no lies
He was married ever
happily after
for all the Tears we cry.

Not only are rock stars fascinated with English Masonic symbols, putting them on their album covers, they incorporate English Masonic doctrine into their lyrics, they stage English Masonic initiation ceremonies in their shows, and many are themselves English Freemasons. For example, Jimmy Page, lead guitarist for Led Zeppelin, in the early 1970s was initiated into the English Masonic Order of the Golden Dawn by Freemason Kenneth Anger. In the 1940s, Anger was initiated into both the Golden Dawn and the O.T.O by none other than Aleister Crowley.

Page, who had praised Crowley as "an unrecognized genius of twentieth century thinking," had become so enamored with the potential of mixing Crowley's magical powers with rock and roll that he purchased Crowley's old mansion, a house located on the shores of the famous Loch Ness and said to be haunted by a death curse. After the purchase, page had a Satanist decorate the inside with occult symbols and then assumed occupancy. Led Zeppelin's drummer, John "Bonzo" Bonham, died in Crowley's mansion, "fueling rumors of sinister overtones resulting from Page's fascination with black magic."

On the Led Zeppelin III album, imprinted into the vinyl band just outside the record's center label, is the phrase, "DO WHAT THOU WILT." This phrase is the whole of the "Law" of the British Ordo Templi Orientis. On the inside cover of the Led Zeppelin IV album is the figure of a hermit.

The Hermit symbolizes occult power and the light of truth. In the hermit's hand is a lantern. The light from within the lantern is in the shape of the six-pointed star, the hexagram of the Priory of Sion, founder of English Freemasonry. The hexagram is also known as the Star of Lucifer."

Two other famous British rock stars initiated into Crowley's Order of the Golden Dawn by Freemason Kenneth Anger are Mick Jagger and Keith Richards of the Rolling Stones. Keith Richards is also a member of Crowley's O.T.O. After his heroin arrest, Richards admitted, "There are black magicians who think we are acting as unknown agents of Lucifer." The Rolling Stones' anthems to Satan, "Sympathy for the Devil" or "Dancing with Mr. D" (the Devil), bear out Richards's comment. And just as Mozart's music conveyed revolutionary propaganda two centuries ago, so too the Rolling Stones continue to spread revolutionary propaganda through their song "Street Fighting Man."

Another admirer of Aleister Crowley is Anton Szandor LaVey, author of The Satanic Bible, and head of the First Church of Satan in California. Co-founder of the Church of Satan with Szandor is Crowley's disciple Freemason Kenneth Anger. Anger's dream was to produce a film glorifying the devil, which would be titled Lucifer Rising. The movie began filming, with the part of Lucifer played by Bobby Beausoleil, a young guitar player with the California rock band, Love. "After filming fora young time, Beausoleil went off the deep end and committed a bestial murder including writing on the wall with his victim's blood." Beausoleil, a was follower of Freemason Charles Manson, who was also a member of Crowley's O.T.O. After Beausoleil was jailed for murder, Kenneth Anger turned to Mick Jagger to play the role of Lucifer. Jagger refused, but he did agree to write the music for it. It finally emerged under the title, Invocation to My Demon Brother.

Satan-Rock

Two other rock groups, Black Sabbath and Blue Oyster Cult, have had great success selling Satan-rock. Black Sabbath's first album was endued Sabbath, Bloody Sabbath. Its cover clearly showed the cross of Christ placed upside down, and displayed the number "666," the mark of the beast.

After a concert in Tulsa, Oklahoma, the Tulsa World music critic confirmed that the subject matter of Black Sabbath's songs are the occult, death and drugs." Not surprisingly, Ozzy Osbourne, former lead singer for Black Sabbath, is devoted to Aleister Crowley, saying Crowley was "a phenomenon of his time."

English rock star Bob Geldof is another Satan-worshipper. When interviewed on CNN Headline News, July 12, 1985, regarding money raised for starving Africans during the Live Aid rock band charity concerts, Geldof made this statement: "With the Devil on my right and the Devil on my left, I would do anything, go to any length to get aid to these people." The next day, July 13, 1985, ABC News lovingly reported on LiveAid: "If humanity decides to get behind a single message, the possibility to communicate that message is limitless. Rock and roll has proven to be the great communicator to the world." A truer statement about rock and roll was never spoken. Fifty million dollars were raised for African aid. And to the eyes of the world, the members of these Devil-worshiping rock bands were portrayed by the media as benevolent young men and women to be honored, followed, and admired by our youth.

For the youth to have a hero, and then mimic his behavior is normal. English Freemasonry is not ignorant of this fact of human existence. By creating "heros" out of rock stars no matter what they do, whatever they like, promote or suggest is a deliberate way of misleading and destroying the young. These "singers" most of whom were, or have become drug addicts themselves promote free sex, drug use, rebellion, and suggest worshiping the devil. Those who listen to their lyrics are in dangerous territory and often follow suit. Jesus Christ, in Matthew 18:67, says of those who would lead astray the young, "But whoso shall offend (apostatize) one of these little ones which believe in me, it were better for him that a millstone were hanged about his neck, and that he drowned in the depth of the sea. Woe unto the world because of offences (stumbling blocks)! for it must needs be that offences come; but woe to that man by whom the offence (entrapment) cometh!"

English Freemason Aldous Huxley has been a "stumbling block" to two generations of our youth.

Huxley's assignment, which he embarked on in the 1930s, was to bring to Hollywood English Freemasonry's Golden Dawn. It spawned what is today known as the rock-drug-sex counterculture, and it has successfully subverted many of our youth, not a few of whom have come from Christian backgrounds, and now have apostatized.

So deeply rooted in our society and culture are the promoters of this counterculture, that our nation is paralyzed from the bottom up, and from the top down. From the bottom up, drugs are under the control of the Masonic Mafia. From the top down, drugs and satanism have been promoted by university professors, the CIA, FBI, and politicians who have served in the Congress and the presidency. Rock groups, however, are the biggest promoters of drugs in our society, and when drug sales decline, the rock groups are used by British Freemasonry to once again increase demand.

How Rock Groups Open New Drug Markets

When the decade of the 1980s began, worldwide drug use among the Youth was at an all-time high. Ronald Reagan had just been elected the fortieth president of the United States, and had declared a war on drugs. Pope John Paul Il had been on Peter's throne since 1978, and had declared war on the Mafia. For the first time in two decades, drug usage was on the decline in both America and Europe, where over ninety percent of illegal drugs are sold. As a result, drug warehouses in the Orient and in South America were filled to overflowing, causing drug Prices to drop and the economies in those Third World nations to decline, which in turn affected the corrupt Euromarket banking industry.

To remedy the problem, the drug barons of London called their groups into action to advertise the drug lifestyle. One example suffice—the 1982 summer European tour of the Rolling stone, led by English Freemasons Mick Jagger and Keith Richards.

The Stones' European tour preempted by protests from the European Anti-Drug Coalition (ADC), which gives us the story. In May 1982, the ADC mobilized tens of thousands of Denmark, Sweden, France, Italy, and West Germany to inform the civic authorities, political and religious forces, and the press of the true implications of the rock group's initiative. It was not a question, said the Coalition, of a cultural event, as the promoters maintained, but of a huge publicity operation by the international narcotics cartel, aimed at recruiting thousands of young people to the drug scene and the Satanic cult of the Rolling Stones. The ADC reported that in economic terms, it was a question of unloading a record crop of 600 tons of opium harvested in the Southeast Asian Golden Triangle, which inventory buildup was perhaps behind the precipitous drop in the prices of heroin on the French markets caused by the simultaneous drop in drug use.

The Stones' tour would have served the purpose of raising the demand for heroin.

As a result of ADC's efforts, Florence, Italy, canceled the Stones concert. Before the Rolling Stones were due to perform at Florence Maria Cristina Fiocchi, president of the Anti-Drug Coalition in Italy, had given a press conference at the Hotel Croce di Malta. Before a crowd of journalists from the principal dailies and the RAI-TV, Italy's national radio-television network, Fiocchi unveiled the links between the drug cartel, the Rolling Stones, English Freemasonry and it sub-societies. "Both Mick Jagger and Keith Richards," said Fiocchi, naming the two most celebrated members of the Rolling Stones, "are members of the Isis-Urania Hermetic Order of the Golden Dawn." The Anti-Drug Coalition had asked for the cancellation of the Naples concert and provided documentation on the Rolling Stones to the Catholic Curia of Naples. Despite the Archbishop's protest to Mayor Valenzi, the concert went ahead.

The concert in Turin was sponsored by Fiat president and 33rd degree Freemason Umberto Agnelli, founding member of the Club of Rome an English Masonic think tank created in 1969 to study how to depopulate the earth by two billion people by the year 2000. Agnelli, sporting a Mohawk haircut at the concert, and Socialist Minister DeMichelis accompanied by his own "groupies," symbolized how political and Masonic collusion had made such a spectacle possible.

Frankfurt, Germany, was another major city that did not take heed of these warnings. The day after Florence cancelled the Stones' concert, scandal broke out in Frankfurt. The Bildzeitung newspaper, with a daily circulation of three million copies, came out With banner headlines that screamed: "At the Stones' Concert: Drugs Like Never Before."

The Frankfurter Rundschau and Frankfurter Allgemeine Zeitung newspaper reported that not only were coolers and tin cans of alcohol all over the concert, but that pills, LSD, hashish, and marijuana circulated peanuts. Ambulances came and went with sirens blaring in competition with the deafening sound of the performers. Frankfurt hospitals refused to give figures on emergency cases, but informed sources reported a hundred or so cases of overdoses; a police press release discussed the complete freedom of pushers to circulate, and the police warned parents not to send their children to the repeat concert.

A Warning to Parents

Parents, if you permit your children to listen to rock and roll music, or attend rock concerts, you are sending them unprotected into a snare devised by English Freemasonry to introduce them to drugs, to incite rebellion against authority, and to worship Satan. In Second Thessalonians 2:1-3, the Apostle Paul warns Christians that before the return of Christ, there will be a falling away, an apostasy, from God. British Masonic rock stars are assisting in bringing the prophesied apostasy to pass.

South-East Asia

Chapter 8

VIETNAM AND THE DRUG WARS

In 1950 the CIA had started to regroup remnants of the defeated Chinese Kuomintang army (KMT) in the Burmese Shan States, where they rapidly became the area's opium barons... The CIA's other allies in the Golden mangle, the Meo, were opium farmers.

Christopher Robbins—Air America

During the 1950s and 1960s, while British Masonic operatives in the academy, music business, and intelligence field were preparing our American youth psychologically and emotionally to enter the rock-drug-sex counterculture, CIA agents were in southeast Asia to guarantee that the increased demand for drugs would be met. In his book Air America (1979), Christopher Robbins presents the thesis that the Vietnam War was a CIA-war largely fought over who would control the opium trade in the Golden Triangle: the communists or the Mafia.

The Golden Triangle is bounded by the rugged Shan hills of northeastern Burma, the mountain ridges of northern Thailand, and the Meo highlands of northern Laos—the world's largest source of opium, morphine, and heroin. "Opium was a fact of economic existence," says Robbins, "as vital as rice, and in Laos it was legal to grow it, transport, and smoke it."

In 1950, as the Chinese Communists moved south and divided Chiang Kai-shek's tattered Chinese Kuomintang (KMT) army east and West, Chiang and his eastern forces fled to the island of

Taiwan and founded the new Republic of China. The western forces of the KMT, isolated and abandoned by both the United States and Chiang Kai-shek, fled south into Burma. Digging themselves into the heart of the opium area to hide from the communists, the KMT expatriates began developing their own defense lines, airstrips, and helicopter landing pads.

One Year earlier in 1949 the U.S. government had contracted British intelligence (SIS) to train its newly recruited CIA agents on how to fight the communists. The man sent to Washington to work in liaison with the CIA and the FBI was Kim Philby, the highly specialized triple agent, who defected to Russia in 1963 to single-handedly topple the Soviet Union. Subsequent events suggest that Philby instructed the Agency in how to fund its covert operations against communism in Southeast Asia with drug money. The CIA held that whatever it took to fund a war against communism was patriotic.

After Philby's tenure with the CIA, many CIA agents were deployed to Burma, Laos, and South Vietnam to assist the ousted KMT Chinese Army in its fight against the Communists. The CIA started to regroup remnants of the KMT in the Burmese Shan States, where they had rapidly become the area's opium barons. The CIA's other ally against the Communists in the Golden Triangle was a local tribe called the Meo, also opium farmers. While the KMT and the Meo fought the war against communism for the CIA, the agency turned a blind eye to their profitable sideline business in opium. Transporting the dope for the dope generals were a number of chartered airlines known collectively as "Air Opium," which were owned and operated by the Corsican Mafia. The receiver and distributor of most of the dope was the American Mafia.

Almost all the KMT opium was flown south in unmarked C-47s to Thailand. From there it was smuggled into South Vietnam where it was sold in opium dens; the proceeds were used to finance Saigon's secret police. Eventually the Corsican Mafia was eliminated by a more ruthless warlord in northwestern Laos, General Ouane Rattikone, who himself was a big-time opium merchant. Without the Corsicans to fly his opium, the general turned to the only air transport available in northern Laos—Air America—owned and operated by the CIA. The CIA had little choice in the matter, for if the Meo's opium was not flown to market, the whole financial apparatus of opium warlords would collapse and their fight against communism would crumble as well. From 1965 to 1971, Air America flew opium from mountain villages north and east of the Plain of Jars in Burma to the headquarters of General Vang Pao at Long Tienge in northern Laos. Paul Withers, a 22 year-old sergeant in the Green Berets, explained the procedure for buying opium when he testified at the Winter Soldier Hearings in Boston in 1971: An Air America plane would arrive at Pak Seng twice a week with supplies and kilo bags of gold dust (from Hong Kong banks) which were given to the Meo in return for their opium. The opium was then loaded onto the planes, each bag marked with the symbol of a particular tribe.

The Kennedys' War Against the Mafia

President John F. Kennedy assumed office in 1961, he planned to eliminate the drug apparatus of America. He appointed as attorney general his brother Robert, who had personally made a commitment to destroy the crime syndicates. The Kennedy brothers planned to replace both J. Edgar Hoover as head of the FBI, and Allen Dulles as head of the CIA and then splinter the CIA into a thousand pieces, replacing it with an alternative intelligence agency. The establishment of this new agency was to be undertaken upon the replacement of Dulles.

From the 1950s, the Kennedy brothers' entire political career had been a war against the Mafia, the CIA, and the FBI. They knew that the Mafia controlled Cuba, the hub for South American drugs distributed to North America. When Robert Kennedy conducted a sustained drive against labor racketeering, Hoover opposed him at every turn. Then, in 1956, as counsel to a Senate committee investigating military procurement, Robert Kennedy learned of the machinations of America's directorate of crime in assisting the Mafia in its attempt to take over the labor unions.

He discovered that a deal had been struck in the early 1940s between New York Mob boss Frank Costello and Freemason J. Edgar Hoover, to allow the Mafia to take over the labor unions in order to keep the communists out. In 1959, Castro's communist revolution in Cuba ousted the Mafia. Immediately the CIA planned what is known as the Bay of Pigs operation to topple Castro and return Cuba to the Mafia. In 1961, when John F. Kennedy moved into the White House and reappointed Dulles as the CIA director, he put a stop to the CIA's LSD experiment, and pulled the plug on Dulles's CIA-backed Bay of Pigs operation, which had been set for April, 1961. Allen Dulles resigned as director of the CIA that autumn.

President Kennedy also knew that the American Mafia was involved in the southeast Asian heroin trade. He was fully aware that the CIA backed Vietnam War was being fought over the control of drugs. He understood that to offer the South Vietnamese our CIA and military assistance against the communists was also to assist the Mafia in their drug business. For these reasons, in the spring of 1963, Kennedy Planned the withdrawal of one thousand troops from Vietnam, beginning December, 1963. He said to his aide, Kenneth O'Donnell, "I'll be damned everywhere as a communist appeaser, but I don't care." Six months after his decision to pull the troops out of Vietnam, Kennedy Was assassinated, and three days after the assassination, Freemason President Lyndon B. Johnson reversed Kennedy's movement toward a military disengagement, permitting American troops to stay in South Vietnam.

Narcotics and the Vietnam War

In 1967, another opium war was being waged in northwestern Laos between the Communists and the CIA-backed army of opium farmers under the control of General Ouane Rattikone. At stake was Burma's opium exports five hundred tons annually, a third of the world's total illicit supply. General Ouane and the CIA won the war against the communists' attempted takeover of their drug business, but their victory precipitated an escalation of the Vietnam War.

Only the British Masonic bankers benefited. For example, not only did the Vietnam War in the south distract from the growth of the drug traffic to the north in the Golden Triangle, the increased production of opium in the north—which was used to fuel the new drug market developing in America by the British rock groups—also added billions of dollars to the bottom line at the British-controlled Hong Kong banks, which funded the entire southeast Asia drug business. As the war in Vietnam intensified, the CIA recruited more and more farmers to grow opium. When rice production declined as a result of the farmers growing the more lucrative opium, the CIA's Air America flew in regular supplies of rice, and flew out the farmers' opium.

In exchange for this service, the opium farmers were expected to furnish young men to fight the communists in Vietnam. Air America helicopters would fly the young men off to battle.

Opium farmers who refused to send their young men to war were warned that unless recruits were forthcoming, Air America's rice drops would stop.

In 1971, the CIA reported that the narcotics output in the largest Of seven factories just north of Ban Houei Sai in northern Laos was "capable of processing some one hundred kilos of raw opium per day." The output from this factory alone produced 3.6 tons of heroin a yean one-third the supply consumed by heroin addicts in America.

During the Vietnam War "the U.S. Bureau of Narcotics was growing increasingly alarmed by the thousands of GIs who had become addicted to Laotian heroin". "The first large influx of heroin to be introduced directly into American military units in Vietnam was in 1968 when a detachment of soldiers, coming from Thailand to South Vietnam to assist American combat forces, brought a supply with them."

One of the soldiers said, "'I just wanted to get out of Nam, and "scag" (heroin) just took me out for a while at least.'" Another soldier, returning home, told army doctors: "'My first tour there in '67, a few of our guys smoked grass. Now the guys walk right in the hootch with a jar of heroin or cocaine. Almost pure stuff. Getting "smack" is like getting a bottle of beer. Everybody sells it. Half my company is on the stuff.'"

When U.S. servicemen began to be pulled out of Vietnam in 1971, the local dealers, all ethnic Chinese tied to the Triads, found their market vanishing. It was only natural that they should turn to the two areas where the servicemen were sent the United States and Western Europe.

In 1972, President Nixon ended the Vietnam War and began his war on Drugs in America, which included sending the Drug Enforcement Agency back to southeast Asia to track down the dope dealers and destroy their factories. For his efforts, Nixon was Watergated.

Statistics of the Drug War

Starting with China in the eighteenth century, destabilization of nations through drug addiction became Great Britain's foreign policy. This foreign policy continues to this day. The danger posed by the international drug trade is well-known to the American government.

Associated Press quoted Vice President George Bush on June 8, 1986, to that effect:

> "For the first time, the U.S. government specifically states that the international drug trade is a national security concern because of its ability to destabilize democratic allies..."

As far back as 1978, statistical data and analysis confirms that the United States is now the prime target of destabilization by the international drug trade—which we have shown can be identified with English Freemasonry. Destabilization begins by weakening an economy—through the loss of dollars sucked out of the economy through the illegal drug trade. In 1978, the worldwide revenue from illicit drug sales was estimated at $200 billion annually, with sixty percent of that gross coming from drugs sold in the United States alone. This means that $120 billion annually is lost from our economy. By 1986, universal illegal drug sales more than doubled, topping $500 billion, with over $300 billion annually drained from the United States economy. These figures were confirmed by many sources throughout the 1980s. U.S. News & world Report, on March 18, 1985, released a new study by Congress, which confirmed that the illegal drug trade had grown dramatically in the United States "at a rate of 10 billion dollars a year since 1978 to an estimated annual gross today of 110 billion dollars. Social costs, which include crime, treatment and drug enforcement, total 100 billion more... The House Narcotics Committee reports that illicit drug use in the U.S. exceeds that of any other industrial nation and is emerging as one of this country's major problems." The percentage of illegal drugs consumed in the United States alone is sixty percent of the world's illegal use approximately $300 billion according to the CBS show, "48 hours on Crack Street", aired September 2, 1986. Again, on February 12, 1987, the Larry Ring Live TV talk show confirmed that the international illegal drug business earns a half trillion dollars annually. And the World Economic Review reported in March 1988 that thirty percent of world trade consists in the selling of illegal dope and arms.

What do all these figures mean? Simply that when cash is paid in illegal transactions for drugs and arms, our government gets no taxes for these transactions, and "flight capital" takes that money out of circulation in our nation.

Should We Legalize Drugs?

Do these statistics provide fuel for legalizing drugs? Some seem to think so. British-born economist Arnold Trebach issued a call in the Wall Street Journal on August 2, 1984, for the legalization of drugs and a "truce" with drug-traffickers. Trebach, director of the National Committee on the Treatment of Intractable Pain and a top propagandist for the legalization of heroin for "medicinal" purposes, wrote:

President Reagan's War on Drugs is a failure. That is not surprising. Every major effort in the 70-year American crusade against these chemicals has also failed… My hope is that when sensible people look at what further escalation of the drug war would really mean, many of them will join me in declaring we have had enough of drug wars and deciding we can rationally co-exist with a good deal of drug use in our society because we do not have the power to make it go away…

One sensible response to our heroin problems would be close to that now practiced in the United Kingdom, where doctors are allowed to provide heroin and a wide variety of other powerful drugs…

The availability of legal marijuana would destroy demand in our largest illegal market.

Of course, some experts argue that less-strict controls will produce an increase in the use, and, eventually, the abuse of drugs.

Perhaps. However, there is strong evidence that there is DRUG a natural WARS to the number of people who will use any drug, whether or not it is freely available.

Where is the "strong evidence" to back up Arnold Trebach's claim that is a "limit to the or people who will any drug?" Today that limit has not yet been reached: some statistics report that eighty percent of school children in some school districts are on drugs, that drug use by teenagers has doubled during the Clinton administration. We will surely lose the war on drugs if drugs are legalized. Only those who are unable to reason will accept Arnold Trebach's premise that legalization will reduce use.

Apparently Trebach did not read the article in The Times, the widely read, influential British newspaper, a month earlier (July 6, 1984) which disapproved his uninformed claims and counsel.

The Times begins a question followed by a series of sarcastic answers: Why not legalize drugs in the USA like they have in England? It would force down the price, thereby taking out the profit for both the smuggler and the pusher. Drug use would die out for lack of good business profits. For what was sold the government would receive sales tax. Addicts, being maintained on low price drugs, would have no need to commit crimes for money to support their habits. Legal drugs would thus reduce if not completely abolish drug-related crime.

After giving the argument of those who are proponents of drug legalization, *The Times* then presented the terrible facts of what legalization of drugs has produced in Great Britain: "Heroin addiction in Britain is more like a plague than an epidemic and threatens the fabric of society," drug treatment experts told the British Medical Association at its annual meeting.

For the first time in this country there is no such place as a drug-free environment.

"The greatest problem in treating addicts is that heroin is now so much cheaper and so easy to obtain," said one expert. He added that people as young as 16 and 17 were becoming dependent upon heroin and that sniffing the drug seemed to be more addictive than injecting it.

"A week's regular use and you are hooked," he said. They spend most of their dole money on heroin, and beg borrow and steal, and in the case of girls—turn to prostitution to pay for their habit.

"We could double the facilities we have available and still not be able to cope," concluded the expert.

Legalizing drugs may be the ultimate goal of Bill Clinton, although he denies it. But Joycelynn Elders, President Clinton's former surgeon general, called for legalization. If we allow legalization, drug use and crime will increase even more rapidly, and even further destabilize our nation.

On February 23, 1995, the president-elect of the American Bar Association, George Bushnell, who in August 1995 takes over the largest organization of lawyers in the U.S., also calls for the legalization of drugs. Bushnell, a trial lawyer in Detroit, says he has held this view for more than thirty years. He parrots the same argument of the uninformed Trebach: "I personally favor decriminalization of all drugs. It takes the profit out of it, which in turn reduces the attractiveness of drug activity among kids. (And) one of the main reasons for crime is that people need money to buy the stuff."

Should We Stop the War on Drugs?

The dramatic drug increases cited earlier began during the presidency of Jimmy Carter and continued through the presidencies of Ronald Reagan and George Bush, who both fought the war on drugs, with a total cost to the taxpayers of nearly $80 billion dollars in one decade. The Clinton White House, however, has all but declared a truce. Clinton's drug czar, Lee Brown, says, "You won't hear us using the metaphor 'drug war.' I don't think we should declare war against our own people." Clinton cut Brown's staff by eighty percent, cut $94 million from the $1.3 billion interdiction budget, and cut $231 million from drug-treatment and prevention programs.

Senator Don Nickles of Oklahoma accused the White House of "surrender" in the drug war.

Meanwhile, at one Washington party, "young administration aides danced and chatted amiably as marijuana fumes wafted indiscreetly through the house. Both the president and vice president have admitted using marijuana".

Bill Clinton is the first Rhodes Scholar to enter the White House. We should expect that Clinton, having been schooled at Oxford by English Masonic professors, and as a member of English Freemasonry's Round Table, Council on Foreign Relations, and Trilateral Commission, is acting on his anglophile education to open our nation to the British Masonic drug barons. This he has done by signing into law in 1993 the North American Free Trade Agreement (NAFTA).

What is likely to follow upon NAFTA is what happened in the nineteenth century to China upon the opening of that country to "free trade." In China, when the "free trade laws" opened the ports to full and unrelenting drug traffic because inspections were outlawed, it was the final blow in English Freemasonry's campaign to destabilize that nation. Likewise, as our borders are gradually opened to the transfer of goods without inspection, we too may face worse destabilization.

Because of Clinton's negligence, the increase of illegal drugs into the United States during the first year of his administration is unprecedented in the history of our nation. According to a survey sponsored by, the Substance Abuse and Mental Health Services Administration of Washington, D.C., since Clinton has taken office, marijuana-related episodes rose 48 percent, cocaine episodes rose 18 percent, and heroin episodes rose 34 percent. Government reports released in the spring of 1994 state that our country is also facing a heroin epidemic this decade, and that the Latin and South American drug cartels are poised to provide the drug.

Why has our nation been singled out for destruction by unseen occultic powers? Simply because we are the last Christian nation and a bastion of freedom. We must be subdued before the one-world Masonic government can be inaugurated—the same government George Orwell described in his book, 1984. When America is unable to fight because of weakness and destabilization caused by drug addiction, we will no longer be a free people. No army need to invade and conquer our land, for we have a Trojan Horse in the White House.

Foreign newspapers are reporting on President Bill Clinton's political corruption, while our own Masonically controlled press remains silent. In February 1995, The Times of London, tied Bill Clinton's rise in politics to illegal drugs:

What is the basic truth of this Whitewater matter? To put it briefly: The state of Arkansas was corrupt the way Mexico is corrupt, long before Bill Clinton entered state politics, long before he was born.

The corruption goes back over a hundred years to the period after the Civil War (when 33rd degree Freemason Albert Pike ran the political machine in Arkansas).

In the 1970s, the corruption came to be financed by drug money, even before Clinton became governor. People got killed; we even Know the names of some of the hit men.

By the early 1980s, drug importation through Arkansas, much of it through Mena airport, reached billions of dollars.

The new narco-millionaires bought political protection by bribery and by financing political campaigns, including Clinton's. They made it their business to involve and implicate their political allies.

They killed dangerous witnesses, including schoolboys and probably including Vincent Foster; his body was moved, his suicide was faked.

As governor, Bill Clinton set up his own unaccounted $700 million ADFA operation, which made loans to his supporters and friends, many of whom subscribed to his political fund.

In the 1980s, Arkansas was awash with cocaine and Money-laundering. It may have been impossible for Bill Clinton to keep his hands clean, but his great mistake was to think that he could go from being governor of Arkansas, a deeply corrupted state, to being U.S. president without the truth emerging.

There is no lack of people who do not want this ugly truth to emerge. The ... national media—the Washington Post, The New York Times, the television network news programs have done their best to turn a blind eye, partly because this is so horrifying a story and partly from political sympathy."

The drug operation headquartered at the Mena airport was used for more than financing a few corrupt politicians and businessmen in Arkansas. It was a CIA operation, according to former CIA contract agent Kenneth C. Bucchi, author of the book C.I.A.: Cocaine In America (1994). Bucchi tells us what was going on at the airport in the mid-1980s, when the CIA was funding the Contras in Nicaragua.

Mena's airstrip is anchored on all corners by pine-smothered mountain ranges. Its remote accessibility, due west of Little Rock near the Oklahoma border, offered a perfect point of cohabitation for drug traffickers and their predators. Large aircraft hangars housed anything from drug planes and their cargo to military weapons destined for Nicaragua. Unrelated CIA operations were simultaneously performing their missions out of this obscure locale in utter anonymity.

Bucchi leaves little doubt that a covert CIA operation funded by illegal drug money, was and is managed out of the Mena, Arkansas, airport' Bucchi's role, along with several other contract agents, was to bring the South American drug cartels to the negotiating table. Their operation, code-named "Pseudo Miranda," used CIA-owned Coast Guard look-alike ships to blow up several cocaine-laden boats and to shoot down as many drug-transporting aircraft as possible to force the South American drug lords to meet in Geneva, Switzerland. In August 1984, the meeting took place at the Hotel Zurich. On one side of the negotiating table sat the drug cartel leaders of South America. On the other side were the CIA and Sicilian Mafia. An agreement was reached that fifty percent of all drugs destined for North America would be airdropped at the Mena airport. From there the Mafia would distribute them throughout the United States. In exchange for the South American drug cartels' cooperation, the CIA would guarantee their aircraft protected passage across U.S. borders. Bucchi gives a brief overview of the operation: Pseudo Miranda aircraft, originating from Colombia, and carrying large quantities of cocaine, would lock onto CIA Long Range Navigation (LORAN) radar. Flying at low level, they could evade US Customs and Defense radar detection systems… When this was not feasible, a shadow aircraft, typically US Air Force with a scheduled flight plan, was used to conceal the radar signature of a drug aircraft flying in close proximity… Once over American soil, they would be intercepted by CIA aircraft and led over Inertial Landing Systems (ILS) radar. Positive identification was established with Identify Friend or Foe (IFF) transponders, that were installed on both trafficker and CIA aircraft. The CIA chase aircraft, having taken the helm, would lead the drug aircraft over a drop zone. The drug plane would then track on the ILS radar beam, typically associated with landing, and release his cargo to agents on the ground. We were those agents. Once we gathered up the cargo, we would transport it to a pre-designated area and fly it to Mena, Arkansas.

With revenue generated from the illegal sale of these drugs, the CIA funded the Contras of Nicaragua in their fight against the communists. This operation flew under the banner of patriotism.

War Against London

Drug merchants are some of the wealthiest men on earth. English Freemasonry and her merchant bankers furnish the drug merchants With offshore banking services to laundering drug money. British bankers are the wealthiest men on earth and in some cases, renowned.

Revelation 18:23 states of Mystery Babylon: "thy merchants were the great men of the earth; for by thy sorceries were all nations deceived." In Greek, merchants means "traveling wholesalers";

sorceries means "the manufacture of mind bending potions"; and deceived means to stray from orthodoxy and piety."

Certainly, English Freemasonry and her worldwide drug operation fit this description. She has caused the nations to stray from the orthodox faith of Christianity. As the most powerful producer and Purveyor of drugs the world has seen, she is certainly a "wholesaler" of addiction and corruption. London manages her drug enterprise from the bottom up through the various groups of ethnic Masonic Mafioso, all of whom are Masons. From the top down, her pernicious doctrines of intellectual and moral relativism, her out and out hedonism, and her contempt for all traditional Western Judeo-Christian religion and inherited values is embraced by our universities, and intellectual and media elite. Further-more, the drug trafficking which afflicts our society is protected by our CIA—a CIA trained by British Masonic intelligence agents.

The frightening solution, in fact the only thing the United States of America can do to stop the drug traffic in our nation is to declare war on England. If England is the Mystery Babylon described by chapters seventeen and eighteen of the book of Revelation, and if the United States is the Beast nation, as we have attempted to prove throughout this three-book series, then Revelation 17:12-13 and 16–18 is prophesying a ten-nation European war against Great Britain—authorized by the United States—for this Scripture reads: And the ten horns which thou sawest are ten kings, which have received no kingdom as yet; but receive power as kings one hour with the beast. These have one mind, and shall give their power and strength unto the beast... And the ten horns which thou sawest upon the beast, these shall hate the whore, and shall make her desolate and naked, and shall eat her flesh and burn her with fire. For God hath put in their hearts to fulfil his will, and to agree, and give their kingdom unto the beast, until the words of God shall be fulfilled. And the woman which thou sawest is that great city, which reigneth over the kings of the earth.

EPILOGUE

> The liberal theory of education is rooted in the Enlightenment notion of human perfectibility through learning evil having come about through ignorance, or adherence to ancient traditions and superstitions. By developing the power of right reason, or improving their material conditions, men were supposed to become better and happier. But the events of this century have rendered faith in progress belief in the progressive improvement of society through the advancement of intelligence—highly questionable.
>
> Lawrence Criner — *The Washington Times*, 1995

If liberal enlightenment was intended to make us perfect, it has failed miserably. Liberalism and the secular education it has fostered and continues to cultivate is the brainchild of Freemasonry, created to incite rebellion against the Holy Trinity and God's Holy Word the Bible.

From the beginning, the Masonic Brotherhood has opposed so called "adherence to ancient traditions and superstitions," which I have shown throughout the three volumes of Scarlet and the Beast are Masonic "catch phrases" for the Brotherhood's concept of Christianity.

Freemasonry teaches that Christian intolerance of other religions has caused all the wars of the last two millenniums. Yet we have witnessed that Freemasonry's intolerance of Christianity has been the secret force behind all political revolutions during the last three centuries, including the two world wars of this century wars so horrific that more people were killed in them than in all previous known wars combined. Freemasonry also teaches that since the beginning of time the God of the Bible and His followers have been responsible for the suppression of science that Masons alone have lost their lives in defense of knowledge, first in the Great Flood, then at the Tower of Babel, and finally during the Inquisition. Freemasonry claims to be the Purveyor of knowledge that has advanced modern science during the last three centuries, giving us the "good life" that we enjoy today. As such, is Freemasonry also willing to accept the responsibility for the weapons of mass destruction that its science has fostered? Scripture speaks of a day when all nations will be at war at Armageddon, bringing life on earth near extinction, unless Christ Himself intervenes to save the human race from itself (Matthew 24:21-22).

But Freemasonry denies God's Word and will never accept the responsibility for the evil it perpetuates. Instead, and under the guise of enlightenment" and "liberty," it has sustained an incessant war against the Holy Trinity. In fact, Freemasonry desires to dethrone God and to enthrone humanity in God's place. Time is its ally. "Gradualism" is its method.

The Masonic conspiracy, which has spanned two centuries, includes the gradual take-over of key positions in business, banking, media, education, religion and government. Freemasonry's plot is dedicated to create a New World Order by giving birth to a new race, a new civilization, and a nonsectarian religion. I shall review the Masonic plan documented in the three volumes of Scarlet and the Beast, then I shall Challenge Christians and patriotic Americans to do what is required to return our nation to its former Christian roots.

The Masonic Plot to De-Christianize America

Freemasonry is not against religion but against sectarianism. The Masonic plan is to eliminate sectarianism by syncretizing all religions into a universal brotherhood at which shrine all men can agree. True Christianity has not, nor will it ever join forces with such a scheme. Therefore, Christianity is the enemy and must be destroyed in America if Freemasonry's plan is to succeed.

The plot to de-Christianize America is recorded in many Scottish Rite documents already quoted.

But one in particular that I shall quote later is both revealing and disturbing Entitled "God's Plan in America," it is in reality Freemasonry's plan for America. The "god" referred to in the article is not the God of the Bible. You will have opportunity to read excerpts from this article, but first I will trace Freemasonry's anti-Christian plot in America.

Freemasonry's war against the God of the Bible first began in Europe following the Masonic revolutions that swept across that continent in the last two centuries. In their wake, the newly formed republics inserted in their constitutions the clause that separated church and state. This was not, however, such an easy task to accomplish in America where 67 percent of the population were professing Christians. The number of Christians in America increased significantly during the Great Awakening of 1730–1740, led by the two popular evangelists, Jonathan Edwards and George Whitefield, and followed by the establishment of congregational, Presbyterian, Methodist, and Baptist churches. By 1787, the year our Constitution became the law of the land, two-thirds of the population professed Christ as Savior. In those early days of the Republic, and for a century following, text books in our rural schools included the Bible.

Colleges such as Harvard, Princeton, and Yale, were founded by Christian benefactors, and presided over by evangelical preachers. The Second Great Awakening (1824–1900), which included much preaching against freemasonry and its dangers to our Christian nation, was led by former Mason Charles G. Finney, president of Oberlin College (Ohio) from 1851–1865, and former 33rd degree Mason Jonathan Blanchard, a Presbyterian minister and president of Wheaton College.

As a result of the anti-Masonic fervor that swept across America throughout the first half of the nineteenth century, Freemasonry went into decline, but it was far from dead. Always sagacious, it had planned for such a day. Like cankerworms that bore into the trunks of trees and destroy a whole forest, Freemasonry had bored into our educational system from its earliest days for the purpose of destroying Christian education. The Masonic Brotherhood of New York began plotting to take over in that state as early as 1795. At the turn of the nineteenth century, Freemasonry founded "free schools" in New York state, which were funded through donations collected by its membership. In the 1820s, New York's key politicians, all of whom were Masons, passed legislation that authorized the State of New York to fund the "free school" system through taxation. This began the state by state Masonic drive to establish the public school system we now know. And it was through this system that the Masons would later begin action to outlaw prayer and Bible-reading in state-controlled schools.

Before Christianity could be removed from the schools, three obstacles had to be overcome.

First, our Constitution did not establish a separation of church and state, nor was such a separation implied. It simply guarantees the freedom to practice any and all religions. Second, the state exes which funded "free schools" also funded parochial schools. Third, school teachers were hired by parents, and for the most part were either of the Christian faith, or had to adhere to and teach Christian principles. Freemasonry set out to hurdle these three obstacles.

In 1857, in an effort to reduce and eventually eliminate Christian teachers from the public schools, the Scottish Rite of Freemasonry created the National Education Association (NEA), a union for school teachers. For the next seventy years the NEA concentrated on recruiting teachers to its ranks. By the 1920s, when Freemasonry controlled a majority of our nation's teachers by their membership in the NEA, the Scottish Rite lobbied our government to create a Department of Education. In that same decade the Scottish Rite also mobilized its entire membership to infiltrate our churches and liberalize them.

In 1935, Freemasonry began its serious drive to de-Christianize the nation by eliminating Christianity from our public institutions—in particular, the schools. Beginning in that year and continuing until his death in 1945, 32nd degree Freemason President Franklin D. Roosevelt appointed to the Supreme Court a majority of justices who were anti-Christian, pro-Communist, radical Masons. In the 1940s, the Scottish Rite led the campaign in Congress against the state funding of parochial schools, and won. During the same decade, the Masonic dominated Supreme Court reinterpreted our Constitution to create the separation of church and state. In the early 1950s, Freemasonry became the force behind the consolidation of public schools in order to wrest control of rural schools from parents. On the eve of that endeavor the Scottish Rite felt the timing appropriate to enlighten the entire body of Masons in the United States of its plot to de-Christianize America through its control of education. Entitled, "God's Plan in America," and published in the Scottish Rite's New Age magazine of September 1950, the plot reads like a Nazi document. As you read this article, notice the New Age overtones. Recognize the anti-biblical dogma; the cursory mention of Christianity, and never the mention of the Name of Jesus Christ. The god of this article is not the God of the Bible. Here is what Freemasonry's god has planned for America:

God's plan is dedicated to the unification of all races, religions and creeds. This plan, dedicated to the new order of things, is to make all things new—a new nation, a new race, a new civilization and a new religion, a nonsectarian religion that has already been recognized and called the religion of "The Great Light."

Looking back into history, we can easily see that the Guiding Hand of Providence has chosen the Nordic people to bring in and unfold the new order of the world.

Records clearly show that 95 percent of the colonists were Nordics—Anglo-Saxons.

Providence has chosen the Nordics because the Nordics have prepared themselves and have chosen God... The Nordics are God's chosen people always looking for more light on the mission of life...

Just as Providence has chosen the Jewish race—the Children of Israel to bring into the world righteousness by carrying the "Ten Commandments" which emphasize "Remember the Sabbath Day and keep it holy," so also Providence has chosen the Nordic race to unfold the "New Age" of the world—a Novus Ordo Seclorum."

One of the first of the Nordics to reach the New World was the Viking, Leif Ericsson.

He sailed from Norway to bring to his people in Ireland a new message, the message of the Christian God. But Providence moves in a mysterious way His wonders to perform, and so Leif the Lucky was sent by Providence to the New World. From the abundance or grapes found there Leif Ericsson called the place Vinland.

It is easy to sense that Leif Ericsson was sent by the Guiding Hand of Providence to bring the Norse spirit of the "All-Father" to the shores of the New World.

The Nordics are the highest branch of the fifth Aryan Civilization. The Latins are the fourth Aryan Civilization, and the American race will be the sixth Aryan Civilization.

This new and great civilization is like an American Beauty rosebud, ready to open and send its wonderful fragrance to all the world.

George Washington, Thomas Jefferson, Benjamin Franklin, John Adams, Thomas Paine and many others of the founders of the new nation in the New World were Nordics.

Thomas Paine, the spark plug of the American Revolution, loved God but hated sectarianism. In "These Art The Times," he wrote: "We have it in our power to begin the world all over again! A situation similar to the present hath not happened since the days of Noah, till now. The Birthday of a New World is at hand." As stated before, God's Plan in America is a nonsectarian plan. Our Constitution is nonsectarian. Our great American Public

Schools—God's chosen schools—are nonsectarian. The Great Spirit behind this great nation is nonsectarian.

Our great American Public Schools have never taken away from any child the freedom of will, freedom of spirit or freedom of mind. That is the divine reason that Great God our King has chosen the great American Public Schools to pave the way for the new race, the new religion and the new civilization that is taking place in America.

Any mother, father or guardian who is responsible for the taking away of freedom of mind, freedom of will or freedom of spirit is the lowest criminal on this earth, because they take away from that child the God-given right to become a part of God's great plan in America for the dawn of the New Age of the world.

This article was one of many published in the Scottish Rite New Age magazine throughout the 1950s to inform Masons of the Masonic plan to abolish sectarian Christianity from the public schools—a plan in the making for one and a half centuries. Not until 1964 was the plan complete.

That year the Masonic-dominated Supreme Court outlawed Bible-reading and prayer in the public schools. The legalization of pornography followed. In 1973, abortion was legalized.

Federal judges are now ruling that state laws against homosexuality are Unconstitutional. Today, adultery if not condoned, is tolerated, and unwed motherhood is no longer a shameful condition. Sexual promiscuity is openly discussed in casual conversations and promoted in song and film. To further encourage hedonism our schools teach "sex educations" and pass out condoms under the guise of "safe sex." The Scriptural prohibition of sex outside of marriage is totally disregarded.

Yes, Freemasonry's policy of "gradualism" has succeeded. The God of the Bible has been thrown out of public schools. He is ignored by much of society. Within one generation following the outlawing of Bible-reading and prayer in public schools, our society went into spiritual decay.

And the Craft's infiltration and liberalization of the mainline churches has made many Christians indifferent to the subsequent decadence and social disorder. A few Christians and a few churches, however, held their Christian banners high, and in the 1960s and following, have founded a number of church-sponsored elementary and secondary schools. Meanwhile, Freemasonry has continued its relentless attack on Christianity by stealing the minds of our youth through music. In the mid-1960s, after Bible-reading and prayer was outlawed in our public schools, English Freemasonry sent her rock and roll stars as emissaries to America to fill the minds of our youth with anthems of rebellion against proper authority and to mock Christian principles. The rock music of the era encouraged experimentation with mind liberating drugs, which caused our children to stray from orthodoxy and piety, and which harmed, ruined, or destroyed many lives and families. The nation's drug problems are today worse than ever.

Satanism is an openly practiced religion. And the new age movement—once practiced in caverns beneath the earth—is the fastest growing religion in America; a religion promoted by Freemasonry.

What does the God of the Bible say about the "good" of Freemasonry, which is identical to the pagan religions of the Old Testament? Leviticus 18 gives the answer. After God had led the Children of Israel out of Egypt, He warned them against living the wicked lifestyle of pagan nations surrounding them. He told them how these wicked nations would be punished for their sins: the earth would vomit them out. He then warned the Israelites that they too would be punished if they followed in the sins of the nations surrounding them. Furthermore, they were not even to permit foreigners in their own land to practice these abominations, lest they be punished along with the foreigners. Listen to God's warning:

The Lord said to Moses, "Speak to the Israelites and say to them: 'I am the Lord your God. You must not do as they do in Egypt, where you used to live, and you must not do as they do in the land of Canaan, where I am bringing you. Do not follow their practices. You must obey my laws and be careful to follow my decrees. I am the Lord your God. Keep my decrees and laws, for the man who obeys them will live by them. I am the Lord.

'No one is to approach any close relative to have sexual relations. I am the Lord...

That is wickedness... Do not have intercourse with your neighbor's wife and defile yourself with her. Do not give any of your children to be sacrificed to Molech, for you must not profane the name of your God. I am the Lord. Do not lie with a man as one lies with a woman; that is detestable. Do not have sexual relations with an animal and defile yourself with it ... that is a perversion. Do not defile yourselves in any of these ways, because this is how the nations that I am going to drive out before you became defiled. Even the land was defiled; so I punished it for its sin, and the land vomited out its inhabitants...

'But you must keep my decrees and my laws. The nativeborn and the aliens living among you must not do any of these detestable things... And if you defile the land, it will vomit you out as it vomited out the nations that were before you... I am the Lord your God.'" (NIV).

We would do well to consider each of these warnings in light of what is happening in the United States of America today:

"No one is to approach any close relative to have sexual relation." A made-for-television movie in November 1991 glorified incest. As I travel throughout the land, I read in local newspapers from coast to coast of children taking their parents to court for incest.

"Do not have intercourse with your neighbor's wife and defile yourself with her." In a recent survey, 50 percent of married men and 30 percent of married women report they have had extramarital affairs. Sex education in our public schools teaches our children how to use condoms for "safe sex" out of wedlock.

"Do not give any of your children to be sacrificed to Molech, for you must not profane the name of your God." Since the Supreme Court legalized abortion in 1973, low estimates calculate that 30,240 unborn children have been "sacrificed to Molech" weekly. As of January 1, 1995, nearly thirty-five million children have been butchered before birth.

"Do not lie with a man as one lies with a woman; that detestable." Homosexuality is taught in many of our public schools as an acceptable lifestyle. Several states have passed "Gay Bill of Rights" laws. One week a year has been set aside for "Gay Pride Week." The Democratic party has declared itself the political party for gays. In 1992, during his first week in office, President Bill Clinton ordered the military to lift its ban on gays. Clinton, keeping his campaign promise to the gay community, appointed at least thirteen known homosexuals and lesbians to various positions in his administration.

"Do not have sexual relations with an animal and defile yourself with it ... that is a perversion." Hard-core pornographic magazines and videos, such as those produced in Northridge, California, and legalized by the Masonic-dominated Supreme Court, picture bestiality. And at least on one occasion, 33rd degree Freemason Aleister Crowley forced his wife to have sex with an animal within the temple walls of his degenerate Masonic sub-lodge.

"But you must keep my decrees and my laws. The nativeborn and the aliens living among you must not do any of these detestable things..." When we declared our independence from Great Britain in 1776, many of the new states declared Christianity the state religion and wrote it into their state constitutions. However, a majority of deistic Masons (53 of 55) wrote and approved the Constitution of the United States of America. No mention of Christ or Christianity can be found in this document. Instead, it guarantees the freedom to practice any and all religion. It is a deistic instrument. Therefore, as more and more immigrants enter our country, pagan religions follow. Today, under the umbrella of the New Age movement, many of these aliens practice the "detestable things" God warned us not to permit.

God's warning applies to Jews and Gentiles alike. He says, "if you defile the land, it will vomit you out as it vomited out the nations that were before you... I am the Lord your God.'"

When our nation was founded, God could have spoken those words to America: "I am the Lord your God." Two hundred years later, we are a nation that has turned its back on the God of the Bible, and we have gone whoring after pagan deities. We have defiled the land with the abominable sins that Almighty God has warned us against. Surely, His judgments will follow, and indeed they have begun. Following is the entire list (with no omissions) of all the natural disasters that have plagued the United States since 1984. These can be verified in the Britannica World Data Annual for each year discussed. I make three observations: (1) notice how the disasters escalate in number, or become more severe each year; (2) notice how the disasters affect America's food supply in our breadbasket states; and (3) notice how the disasters are becoming more costly, bankrupting many insurance companies, and burdening our government as it plunges deeper into debt to bail out states unable to bear the costs of recovery.

1984: On February 4, Arctic cold and blowing snow invaded the country from Canada, immobilizing many of the Plains states. On February 28, a deadly winter storm crippled cities from St. Louis to Detroit to Buffalo, forcing airports, schools, offices, and factories to close for two days in many major cities. On March 9, a powerful winter storm that blew in from Canada was dubbed the "Alberta Clipper" and blasted the Northeast with up to a foot of snow, making roads impassable. On March 14, the worst March snowstorm of the century dumped from one to three feet of snow from eastern New York to Maine. From March 1903, heavy snowstorms in the Rocky Mountains precipitated severe thunderstorms accompanied by hail in Texas and Oklahoma. On March 28, a string of tornadoes cut a 300-mile swath of destruction across South Carolina and North Carolina. One of the worst natural disasters in the century, the tornadoes killed 70 people and caused property damage in the billions of dollars. On April 21, tornadoes spawned by severe thunderstorms ravaged northern Mississippi. On April 26, a deadly tornado flattened more than half the homes and businesses in Morris, Oklahoma, claiming the lives of eleven persons. From May 6–9, severe thunderstorms complicated by tornadoes caused widespread flooding in the states of Ohio, Kentucky, Tennessee, Louisiana, Maryland, and West Virginia. At least 14 persons were killed and some 6,000 others were left homeless. On May 27, an overnight downpour of up to a foot of rain in Tulsa, Oklahoma, flooded more than 2,100 homes and left thousands homeless. In late-May and early-June, a slow moving rainstorm dumped 9.2 inches of rain, causing widespread flooding in the Northeast. Eighteen deaths were attributed to the storm and thousands were left homeless. On June 8, a killer storm spawned 49 tornadoes that swept through the Plains and upper Midwest, where a total of 16 persons were killed. Barneveld, Wisconsin, was completely demolished by a twister that flattened ninety homes, thirty businesses and public buildings. The second half of the year remained calm.

1985: In late January, a nationwide cold wave set record temperatures in the East and Southeast, severely damaging Florida citrus crops. It was blamed for at least 128 deaths. From January 30 through February 2, a widespread storm system that set record low temperatures from Michigan to Texas and dumped snow from the Southwest to England was blamed for the deaths of 24 persons. On May 31, a 300-mile frontal system crossing Ohio, Pennsylvania and New York, spawned a pack of killer tornadoes that left a swath of death and destruction. At least 88 persons were known dead, hundreds were injured, and whole towns were virtually wiped out by the roaring twisters. On August 2, a brutal thunderstorm, accompanied by damaging winds and hail, dumped six inches of rain in four hours on Cheyenne, Wyoming, and caused heavy flooding. In late October, tropical

Storm Juan caused four days of heavy flooding in Louisiana, $1 billion in damage, and at least seven deaths. In early November, a staggering 20 inches of rainfall in a 12-hour period caused swollen rivers in West Virginia, Virginia, Maryland, and Pennsylvania to overflow their banks. Thousands of homes were destroyed and at least 49 persons were killed.

Property damage in the Virginias alone was estimated at $500 million. In mid-November, a winter snowstorm in the northwest was blamed for the deaths of at least 33 persons. Florida was pounded by Hurricane Kate from November 19–21. At least 24 persons were killed. In early December, an early winter snowstorm pummeled the midwestern states, causing 19 deaths.

1986: From February 13–14, brutal and punishing Pacific storms lashed the western states, producing flooding, mud slides, high winds, and avalanches. Hardest hit was northern California where 12,335 houses and 927 businesses were damaged or destroyed. On May 30, severe thunderstorms triggered mud slides and flash floods in the central mountains of Pennsylvania.

The rest of the year was calm. This was an election year—a year we had a chance to vote out a liberal congress. We failed to rise to the occasion.

1987: On January 22, a deadly blast of arctic air accompanied by a blizzard struck the East Coast from Maine to Florida and claimed at least 37 lives. On February 16, an ice storm in North Carolina caused hundreds of traffic accidents, with 17 persons killed. On May 22, a tornado ravaged the small farming town of Saragosa, Texas, and leveled a community house where some 100 persons had gathered for a preschool graduation ceremony. On July 17, a bus and a van carrying members from a church camp stailed on a bridge and were swept away by swollen waters from the Guadeloupe river in Comfort, Texas. From late-July through early-August, a blistering heat wave scorched the central part of the nation, which led to the deaths of at least 80 persons. On October 1, a powerful earthquake near Los Angeles, measuring

6.1 on the Richter scale, triggered fires, shattered glass from skyscrapers, and caused more than $100 million in damages. From December 12 through 16, a major snowstorm packing high winds closed airports and schools, knocked down power lines, and spawned tornadoes in Arkansas. Seventy-three deaths were blamed on the storm, which pummeled parts of Wisconsin, Michigan, Missouri, Illinois, Indiana, Minnesota, Ohio, Iowa, and Kansas.

1988: During the summer about 35 percent of the United States experienced severe drought.

The midwestern states, the bread basket of America, suffered the worst dry conditions since the Dust Bowl of 1934. Major crop areas received less than half the normal rainfall during the critical growing period from April through June. As if God was giving us an opportunity to repent, the rest of the year was calm. It was an election year—the first election year that a presidential candidate (Pat Robertson) openly declared that if elected Jesus Christ would be Lord of his administration. We failed to rise to the occasion.

1989: In January, a bone-chilling storm system gripped the Midwest and the East and delivered snow and strong winds that paralyzed much of the South. In February, a major snowstorm pummeled the South and the Northeast with up to a foot of snow. On May 6, a storm that spawned tornadoes and precipitated flooding roared through Oklahoma, Texas, Louisiana, South Carolina, North Carolina, and Virginia. From September 17–21, Hurricane Hugo, one of the nations most fierce storms in a decade, wreaked a path of destruction through South and North Carolina, with damage estimated in the billions of dollars. On October 17, during the World Series, an earthquake measuring 7.1 on the Richter scale hit the San Francisco Bay area, inflicting billions of dollars in damage.

1990: In early to mid-May, Texas, Oklahoma, Louisiana, and Arkansas suffered severe rainstorms, which produced massive flooding that reached rooftop levels, taking lives and causing millions of dollars in damage. At least 117 counties in the four affected states were declared disaster areas. On June 2 and 3, a spate of deadly tornadoes descended on Indiana, Illinois, and Wisconsin, taking lives and causing millions of dollars in damage. On June 14, severe thunderstorms precipitated a frightening flash flood in Shadyside, Ohio that sent a ten-foot wall of water surging through the creek-laced valley. On August 28, a ferocious tornado developed so quickly in Plainfield, Illinois, that it was undetected by weather radar and left a path of destruction some eight miles long, taking lives and causing millions in damage. This was an election year—a year we had an opportunity to vote out a liberal Congress. We failed to rise to the occasion.

1991: Prom March 28–29, severe thunderstorms accompanied by high winds through Arkansas, Louisiana, Mississippi, Alabama, Georgia, South Carolina, North Carolina, and Virginia, taking lives causing millions of dollars in damage. On April 26, an onslaught of more than 70 tornados swept through Kansas and six other states, carving paths of destruction and claiming lives along the way. Hurricane Bob pummeled the eastern coast from August 18–20, taking lives and inflicting millions of dollars in damage on the heavily populated states of North Carolina, Maine, Massachusetts, Connecticut, New York, and Rhode Island. From December 21–22, massive flooding throughout much of eastern Texas followed five days of torrential downpours, causing deaths and millions of dollars in damage.

1992: In mid-February, relentless rainstorms hit California for nearly a week, precipitating widespread flooding in Los Angeles and Ventura counties, and causing $23 million in damage.

On April 29, four days following a massive pro-abortion rally held by gays in Philadelphia, an earthquake hit northern California with a magnitude of 6.9 on the Richter scale. On June 28 (Gay Pride Day), as gays were celebrating their sin by parading naked through the streets of major cities in the U.S., two earthquakes hit California; one 7.6 and the other 6.5 on the Richter scale.

August 23–26: Hurricane Andrew, the costliest natural disaster in U.S. history, struck the Bahamas before rampaging across southern Florida, where it virtually annihilated the towns of Homestead and Florida City, with wind gusts up to 264 mp/h. In Florida, 63,000 homes were destroyed, three million homes and businesses were without power. Damage totaled over $20 billion. In Louisiana, the damage caused by Andrew cost $300 million, which included half of the state's sugar crop; 44,000 persons left homeless.

November 21–23: as many as 45 freak tornadoes zigzagged across eleven states from Texas to as far north as Ohio, creating massive destruction. December 10–11: a brutal and deadly winter storm in the northeastern U.S. was designated an extratropical cyclone by the U.S. National Weather Service. It dumped four feet of snow, and packed strong winds that inflicted some $10 million in damages on New Jersey's Atlantic City. This was an election year—the year the Democratic party declared it "was the party for gays." Again, we failed to rise to the occasion.

We elected an antichrist president who appointed many gays and communists to vital positions in his administration. Recently, Bill Clinton sent to the U.S. Senate for ratification a United Nations treaty, called the "Convention on Biological Diversity." Among other things, the treaty proposes "to make nature worship a state religion."

1993: From January 7–20, two weeks of relentless pounding rain caused massive mud slides and severe flooding in southern California, killing 30 persons and leaving more than 1,000 homeless.

March 12–15: a ferocious storm hit the Eastern Seaboard. Billed as the Blizzard of '93, it produced record-breaking bitter-cold temperatures, dumping tons of snow from Alabama to Maine, while spawning tornadoes in Florida, where residents were still recovering from the 1992 destruction caused by Hurricane Andrew. The storm claimed the lives of 238 persons, trapped some 100 hikers and several campers, and spread destruction as far north as Canada and as far south as Cuba. Damage estimates reached $1 billion. From mid-June through August, a stormy weather front stagnated for weeks over the Midwest, causing the worst flooding in U.S. history in the states of Illinois, Iowa, Kansas, Minnesota, Missouri, Nebraska, North Dakota, South Dakota, and Wisconsin. The Great Flood of '93 caused an estimated $12 billion in damages, including $200 million to rail lines and bridges and $8 billion in crop damages. In early July, a searing week-long heat wave, with punishing temperatures over 100 degrees, claimed lives in the Northeast. From late October to early November, southern California was seared by a series of wildfires driven by the Santa Ana winds. At least 152,000 acres were destroyed.

1994: In mid-January, a bitter arctic cold wave stretched from the Midwest to the Eastern Seaboard and paralyzed the regions with temperatures plummeting to record-breaking lows.

More than 140 deaths were attributed to the deep freeze. On January 17, a strong pre-dawn earthquake of a magnitude of 6.8 on the Richter Scale violently shook Los Angeles, killing 61 persons, injuring more than 9,000, and resulting in $20 billion in damage. Northridge, the hardest hit area, and closest to the epicenter in the San Fernando Valley, is where most of our nation's pornography videos are made. On March 27, a series of violent thunderstorms and ferocious tornadoes wreaked widespread destruction across Tennessee, Alabama, Georgia, North Carolina, and South Carolina, killing at least 42 persons. In early July, Tropical Storm Alberto stalled over Georgia, Alabama, and Florida, dumping as much as 24 inches of rain in some areas. Thirty-one deluged counties across the three states were declared federal disaster areas. From October 16–19, as much as 30 inches of rain soaked Houston, Texas, causing massive flooding of the San Jacinto River Basin, and submerging homes and highways. Tropical Storm Gordon unleashed its fury from November 13–19, heading northeast across southern Florida, and crossing into the North Atlantic before making a U-turn back to Florida. The zigzagging storm Claimed the of at least 537 persons in the Caribbean islands and Florida, and cost at least

$200 million in damages in Florida alone. This was an election year—a year we rose to the occasion and elected a conservative Congress.

Yes, the land is vomiting us out, because we as a nation have not heeded God's warning to abandon our practice of these abominable sins. If we persist in our disobedience and rebellion against God, we can expect natural disasters to continue and even escalate, further destroying our land and our economy. Thomas Jefferson foresaw the day that moral decay might destroy America. He issued this warning two centuries ago:

Yes, we did produce a near perfect Republic. But will they keep it, or will they, in the enjoyment of plenty, lose the memory of freedom? Material abundance without character is the surest way to destruction.

Alexis de Tocqueville, a French political philosopher who visited the United States while we were yet a young nation, left a similar warning. He came specifically to America to learn what magic quality enabled a handful of people to defeat the mighty British Empire twice in 35 years. He looked for the greatness of America in her harbors and rivers, her fertile fields and boundless forests, mines and other natural resources. He studied America's schools, her Congress and her matchless Constitution without comprehending America's power. Not until he went into the churches of America and heard pulpits "aflame with righteousness" did he understand the secret of her genius and strength. De Tocqueville returned to France and wrote: America is great because America is good, and if America ever ceases to be good, America will cease to be great.

The soul of America is no longer good. Yet, there are good people in America. What are we to do? The answer is not to take up arms against our Masonic-controlled government. Our answer is to be found in an infinitely merciful God, Who is willing to forgive if we simply repent.

Repentance begins at the house of God with God's people, both Jews and Christians alike. In Second Chronicles 7:14, God gives us the four step formula for a healed land: If my people, which are called by my name, shall humble themselves, and pray, and seek my face, and turn from their wicked ways; then will I hear from heaven, and will forgive their sin, and will heal their land.

Pastors, priests, and rabbis, preach this message to your people, and lead by example.

Second, God pleads with His people in Revelation 18:4-6 to disassociate themselves from Mystery Babylon (Freemasonry), or suffer the consequences. The Apostle John records Christ's Words:

> And I heard another voice from heaven, saying, Come out of her, my people, that ye be not partakers of her sins, and that ye receive not of her plagues. For her sins have reached unto heaven, and God hath remembered her iniquities. Reward ... her double according to her works: in the cup which she hath filled fill to her double.

Dear Christian brothers and Jewish friends who have joined hands with Freemasonry, the implication is clear in the above verse that you will receive the plagues allotted to Freemasonry if you stubbornly and obstinately remain in fellowship in the lodge. Moreover, these plagues will be transferred to your family, and they too will suffer affliction. According to Zechariah 5, your membership in the lodge has caused a curse to enter your house—a curse that will destroy your family and your children. There is a cure: Renounce your affiliation with Freemasonry today by following the instruction set forth at the end of chapter five and in appendix 8 of Scarlet and the Beast, volume one. God will heal your family and grant you a pardon from future plagues that will be visited upon Freemasonry and its membership.

After repentance, pray for our political leaders to repent. Write them—inform them that you are praying for our nation to repent. Ask them to repent with you. Specify how they can do this: by returning our nation to the days when pornography, abortion, and homosexuality, etc. were illegal; by restoring prayer and Bible-reading in our public schools as a sanctioned, daily practice.

Compel our legislators to remove "values clarification" from our schools and once again allow the Ten Commandments to be taught. Require teachers to teach our children biblical ethics.

Remind your congressman and our president that your vote counts. Consider the actions of our leaders. Then vote only for those leaders whose rhetoric and actions are both godly. Do not vote for those leaders whose rhetoric pleases, but whose actions are ungodly. They are liars and deceivers. We proved the power of our vote in the 1994 congressional elections. Let us keep the momentum going.

OTHER TITLES

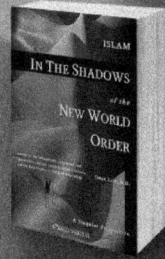

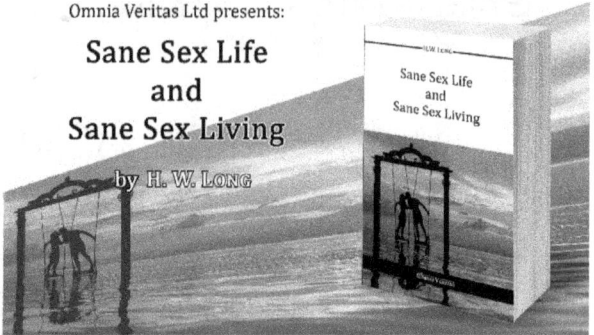

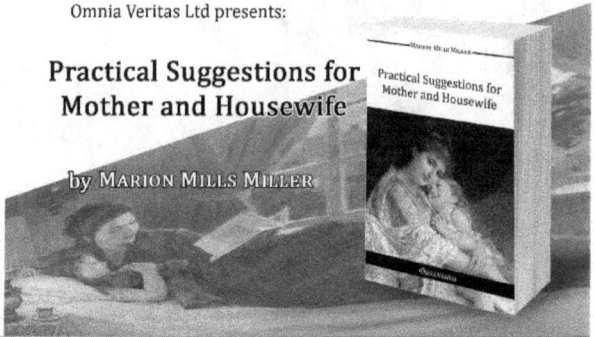

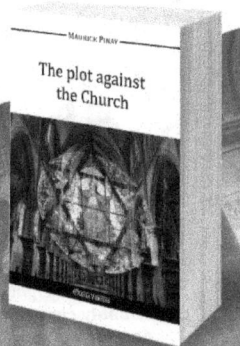

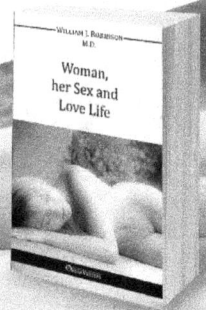

Omnia Veritas Ltd presents: **The History of Money**

It is fascinating and almost magical how money appeared on our planet...

Most people don't realise that the issuing of money is a private business...

Omnia Veritas Ltd presents: **THE LEGALIZED CRIME OF BANKING** by SILAS WALTER ADAMS

A free press is the guardian genius of a just, honest, and humane democracy, as Lincoln put it:

"To sin by silence when they know they should protest, makes cowards of men."

"There is a great deal of difference between a **moral wrong** and a **legal right**"

A liberating and much acclaimed book on the Federal Reserve system!

Omnia Veritas Ltd presents: **The Servile State** by HILAIRE BELLOC

"If we do not restore the Institution of Property we cannot escape restoring the Institution of Slavery; there is no third course."

Surprisingly compelling and enlightening, an **indispensable** of any **serious economic study**

Hilaire Belloc's classic *in a new edition!*

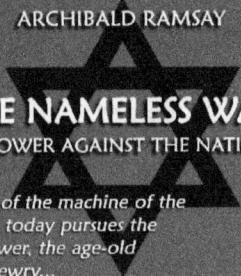

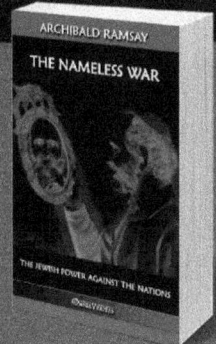

www.ingramcontent.com/pod-product-compliance
Lightning Source LLC
Chambersburg PA
CBHW061725270326
41928CB00011B/2122